TEACHER'S PET PUBLICATIONS

LITPLAN TEACHER PACK
for
Roll of Thunder, Hear My Cry
based on the book by
Mildred Taylor

Written by
Mary B. Collins

© 1996 Teacher's Pet Publications
All Rights Reserved

This **LitPlan** for Mildred Taylor's
Roll of Thunder, Hear My Cry
has been brought to you by Teacher's Pet Publications, Inc.

Copyright Teacher's Pet Publications 1996
11504 Hammock Point
Berlin MD 21811

Only the student materials in this unit plan
such as worksheets, study questions, assignment sheets and tests
may be reproduced multiple times for use in the purchaser's classroom.

For any additional copyright questions,
contact Teacher's Pet Publications.

www.tpet.com

TABLE OF CONTENTS - *Roll of Thunder, Hear My Cry*

Introduction	5
Unit Objectives	8
Reading Assignment Sheet	9
Unit Outline	10
Study Questions (Short Answer)	13
Quiz/Study Questions (Multiple Choice)	21
Pre-reading Vocabulary Worksheets	39
Lesson One (Introductory Lesson)	53
Nonfiction Assignment Sheet	55
Oral Reading Evaluation Form	57
Writing Assignment 1	60
Writing Assignment 2	68
Writing Assignment 3	75
Vocabulary Review Activities	66
Extra Writing Assignments/Discussion ?s	64
Unit Review Activities	76
Unit Tests	79
Unit Resource Materials	109
Vocabulary Resource Materials	123

A FEW NOTES ABOUT THE AUTHOR
MILDRED D. TAYLOR

TAYLOR, MILDRED. Born in Jackson, Mississippi, Mildred Taylor spent most of her childhood in Toledo, Ohio. She attended both the University of Toledo and the University of Colorado. In between her studies at the two universities, Mildred Taylor spent two years with the Peace Corps in Ethiopia.

Besides *Roll of Thunder, Hear My Cry*, a Newbery Medal winner, Ms. Taylor has also written *The Gold Cadillac, Let the Circle Be Unbroken,* and *Song of the Trees* (winner of a Council on Interracial Books Award and New York Times Outstanding Book of the Year for 1975).

INTRODUCTION

This unit has been designed to develop students' reading, writing, thinking, and language skills through exercises and activities related to *Roll of Thunder, Hear My Cry* by Mildred D. Taylor. It includes twenty lessons, supported by extra resource materials.

The **introductory lesson** introduces students to the theme of responsibility/duty. Following the introductory activity, students are given a transition to explain how the activity relates to the book they are about to read. Following the transition, students are given the materials they will be using during the unit. At the end of the lesson, students begin the pre-reading work for the first reading assignment.

The **reading assignments** are approximately thirty pages each; some are a little shorter while others are a little longer. Students have approximately 15 minutes of pre-reading work to do prior to each reading assignment. This pre-reading work involves reviewing the study questions for the assignment and doing some vocabulary work for 8 to 10 vocabulary words they will encounter in their reading.

The **study guide questions** are fact-based questions; students can find the answers to these questions right in the text. These questions come in two formats: short answer required or multiple choice. The best use of these materials is probably to use the short answer version of the questions as study guides for students (since answers will be more complete), and to use the multiple choice version for occasional quizzes. If your school has the appropriate machinery, it might be a good idea to make transparencies of your answer keys for the overhead projector.

The **vocabulary work** is intended to enrich students' vocabularies as well as to aid in the students' understanding of the book. Prior to each reading assignment, students will complete a two-part worksheet for approximately 8 to 10 vocabulary words in the upcoming reading assignment. Part I focuses on students' use of general knowledge and contextual clues by giving the sentence in which the word appears in the text. Students are then to write down what they think the words mean based on the words' usage. Part II nails down the definitions of the words by giving students dictionary definitions of the words and having students match the words to the correct definitions based on the words' contextual usage. Students should then have an understanding of the words when they meet them in the text.

After each reading assignment, students will go back and formulate answers for the study guide questions. Discussion of these questions serves as a **review** of the most important events and ideas presented in the reading assignments.

After students complete reading the work, a lesson is devoted to the **extra discussion questions/writing assignments**. These questions focus on interpretation, critical analysis and personal response, employing a variety of thinking skills and adding to the students' understanding of the novel.

There is a **vocabulary review** lesson which pulls together all of the fragmented vocabulary lists for the reading assignments and gives students a review of all of the words they have studied.

The **group activity** which follows the discussion questions has students working in small groups to discuss the main themes of the novel. Using the information they have acquired so far through individual work and class discussions, students get together to further examine the text and to brainstorm ideas relating to the themes of the novel.

The group activity is followed by a **reports and discussion** session in which the groups share their ideas about the themes with the entire class; thus, the entire class is exposed to information about all of the themes and the entire class can discuss each theme based on the nucleus of information brought forth by each of the groups.

There are three **writing assignments** in this unit, each with the purpose of informing, persuading, or having students express personal opinions. The first assignment is to inform: students identify the distinctly different personalities of the Logan children. The second assignment is to persuade: students pretend to be Mary Logan persuading a neighbor to boycott Mr. Wallace's store. The third assignment is to give students a chance to express their own ideas: students decide what their aspirations are for the future and create a plan for achieving their goals.

In addition, there is a **nonfiction reading assignment**. Students are required to read a piece of nonfiction related in some way to *Roll of Thunder, Hear My Cry*. After reading their nonfiction pieces, students will fill out a worksheet on which they answer questions regarding facts, interpretation, criticism, and personal opinions. During one class period, students make **oral presentations** about the nonfiction pieces they have read. This not only exposes all students to a wealth of information, it also gives students the opportunity to practice **public speaking**.

The **review lesson** pulls together all of the aspects of the unit. The teacher is given four or five choices of activities or games to use which all serve the same basic function of reviewing all of the information presented in the unit.

The **unit test** comes in two formats: multiple choice or short answer. As a convenience, two different tests for each format have been included.

There are additional **support materials** included with this unit. The **extra activities section** includes suggestions for an in-class library, crossword and word search puzzles related to the novel, and extra vocabulary worksheets. There is a list of **bulletin board ideas** which gives the teacher suggestions for bulletin boards to go along with this unit. In addition, there is a list of **extra class activities** the teacher could choose from to enhance the unit or as a substitution for an exercise the teacher might feel is inappropriate for his/her class. **Answer keys** are located directly after the **reproducible student materials** throughout the unit. The student materials may be reproduced for use in the teacher's classroom without infringement of copyrights. No other portion of this unit may be reproduced without the written consent of Teacher's Pet Publications, Inc.

UNIT OBJECTIVES - *Roll of Thunder, Hear My Cry*

1. Through reading Mildred D. Taylor's *Roll of Thunder, Hear My Cry*, students will study the themes of injustice, naivete, revenge, friendship, pride/dignity, and duty/responsibility.

2. Students will demonstrate their understanding of the text on four levels: factual, interpretive, critical and personal.

3. Students will define their own viewpoints on the aforementioned themes.

4. Students will be exposed to a different era of American life, showing many of today's conflicts are not new; they are rooted in our American past.

5. Students will see that each of our daily life experiences changes us and shapes our thoughts and feelings.

6. Students will be given the opportunity to practice reading aloud and silently to improve their skills in each area.

7. Students will answer questions to demonstrate their knowledge and understanding of the main events and characters in *Roll of Thunder, Hear My Cry* as they relate to the author's theme development.

8. Students will enrich their vocabularies and improve their understanding of the novel through the vocabulary lessons prepared for use in conjunction with the novel.

9. The writing assignments in this unit are geared to several purposes:
   a. To have students demonstrate their abilities to inform, to persuade, or to express their own personal ideas
      NOTE: Students will demonstrate ability to write effectively to <u>inform</u> by developing and organizing facts to convey information. Students will demonstrate the ability to write effectively to <u>persuade</u> by selecting and organizing relevant information, establishing an argumentative purpose, and by designing an appropriate strategy for an identified audience. Students will demonstrate the ability to write effectively to <u>express personal ideas</u> by selecting a form and its appropriate elements.
   b. To check the students' reading comprehension
   c. To make students think about the ideas presented by the novel
   d. To encourage logical thinking
   e. To provide an opportunity to practice good grammar and improve students' use of the English language.

READING ASSIGNMENT SHEET - *Roll of Thunder, Hear My Cry*

Date Assigned	Chapters Assigned	Completion Date
	1-2	
	3-4	
	5-6	
	7-8	
	9-10	
	11-12	

UNIT OUTLINE - *Roll of Thunder, Hear My Cry*

1 Introduction PV 1-2	2 Read 1-2	3 Study ?s 1-2 PVR 3-4	4 Study ?s 3-4 PVR 5-6	5 Study ?s 5-6 Writing Assignment 1 PVR 7-8
6 Study ?s 7-8 PVR 9-10	7 Quiz/?s 9-10 PVR 11-12	8 Study ?s 11-12 Extra ?s	9 Vocabulary	10 Writing Assignment 2
11 Group Activity	12 Discussion	13 Library	14 Nonfiction Discussion	15 Speaker
16 Shopping Spree	17 Writing Assignment 3	18 Writing	19 Review	20 Test

Key: P = Preview Study Questions   V = Prereading Vocabulary Work   R = Read

STUDY GUIDE QUESTIONS

SHORT ANSWER STUDY GUIDE QUESTIONS - *Roll of Thunder, Hear My Cry*

Chapter 1
1. Why was Little Man lagging behind?
2. Why was Stacey in a bad mood?
3. What made Papa need to find work?
4. What happened to the Berrys?
5. How did T.J. get out of his punishment?
6. Who was Jeremy?
7. Describe Cassie.
8. Why was the prospect of having readers exciting?
9. Why did Cassie and Little Man refuse to take their readers?
10. How did Mary Logan react to Daisy's news about the children's refusal to accept the books?

Chapter 2
1. Describe Mr. Morrison.
2. What did Mr. Morrison tell the Logans about his past?
3. How did the congregation feel about the burnings?
4. Why didn't Papa want the children to go to the Wallaces' store?

Chapter 3
1. What was the problem with the Jefferson Davis school bus?
2. Why did the Logan children dig a hole in the road?
3. How did Mama and Big Ma react to the news of the stuck bus?
4. Who were the "riders," and what were they doing?

Chapter 4
1. Why was Cassie upset?
2. Why were the night men actually out the night Cassie saw them?
3. Why had Papa hired Mr. Morrison?
4. Why did Stacey get whipped?
5. What did Mama do when she found out that the children had been at the Wallaces' store?
6. Why did Mama try to convince Mr. Turner to stop shopping at the Wallaces' store?

Chapter 5
1. Why was Cassie disappointed in Strawberry?
2. Why did Big Ma park her wagon away from the entrance?
3. Why did Cassie like Mr. Jamison?
4. What made Cassie yell at Mr. Barnett?

Chapter 6
1. Why was Cassie mad at Big Ma?
2. Identify Uncle Hammer.
3. What explanation did Mama give Cassie for Mr. Simms' actions?
4. What happened to Stacey's new coat? What was Uncle Hammer's reaction?
5. How did Uncle Hammer and the Logans surprise the Wallaces?

Chapter 7
1. Why were the last few days of school before Christmas difficult for Cassie?
2. Why didn't Papa want to back people's credit with his land?
3. What did Jeremy give Stacey?
4. What papers did Big Ma sign?
5. Why did Mr. Jamison want to back the people's credit?
6. What did Mr. Granger say to the Logans?

Chapter 8
1. What was Cassie doing for Lillian Jean?
2. Why did Cassie take Lillian Jean into the woods?
3. Why did Mama lose her teaching job?
4. Who sicced the school board on Mama?
5. What was T.J.'s punishment?

Chapter 9
1. What were R.W. and Melvin doing to T.J.?
2. Why were Mr. Avery and Mr. Lanier not going to shop in Vicksburg anymore?
3. Why were Mr. Morrison, Papa and Stacey late coming home?
4. Who shot Papa and tried to kill Mr. Morrison?

Chapter 10
1. Why didn't Papa want to borrow money from Hammer?
2. How did Mr. Morrison avoid Kaleb Wallace?
3. Why did the Logans finally have to depend on Uncle Hammer for money?
4. Where did Hammer get the money for the mortgage?
5. How had T.J. changed?

Chapter 11
1. What happened to T.J.?
2. Why did Stacey send Cassie and her brothers home?

Chapter 12
1. What stopped the mob?
2. How did the fire start?
3. What happened to T.J.?
4. Why did Cassie cry?

ANSWER KEY SHORT ANSWER STUDY GUIDE QUESTIONS
Roll of Thunder, Hear My Cry

Chapter 1
1. Why was Little Man lagging behind?
   He didn't want to get dirt on his clothes, so he had to walk gingerly.

2. Why was Stacey in a bad mood?
   He had to be in his mother's class that year.

3. What made Papa need to find work?
   In 1930 the price of their cotton crop dropped, so money was short.

4. What happened to the Berrys?
   They were burned when a white man set fire to them.

5. How did T.J. get out of his punishment?
   He told his mother that Claude went to the Wallaces' store and that he had to go get Claude.

6. Who was Jeremy?
   He was a shy boy who was beaten by his parents for associating with Cassie and her brothers.

7. Describe Cassie.
   Cassie is a fourth-grade student who despises dressing up and sticks up for her own rights.

8. Why was the prospect of having readers exciting?
   Most of the children had never had books other than a Bible before.

9. Why did Cassie and Little Man refuse to take their readers?
   In the front of the books, the black students were called "nigra," and the books were handed-down leftovers in very poor condition from the white school.

10. How did Mary Logan react to Daisy's news about the children's refusal to accept the books?
    She understood her children very well and politely dismissed Daisy's anger.

Chapter 2
1. Describe Mr. Morrison.
   He was a tall, formidable man whom Papa hired as a farm hand.

2. What did Mr. Morrison tell the Logans about his past?
>He wanted them to know that he had been in trouble for beating up a white man.

3. How did the congregation feel about the burnings?
>They were disgusted about the burnings. They felt that is was wrong and not enough w as being done about it.

4. Why didn't Papa want the children to go to the Wallaces' store?
>People went there to drink and carouse, and the children who frequented the place usually ended up in trouble. It wasn't a wholesome place for young people.

Chapter 3

1. What was the problem with the Jefferson Davis school bus?
>Every day the driver would run the black children off of the road just for "fun" and so the white children on the bus could jeer at them.

2. Why did the Logan children dig a hole in the road?
>They wanted to get even with the Jefferson Davis school bus driver and kids. By digging a hole in the road, they hoped to cause the bus to at least get stuck (which it did).

3. How did Mama and Big Ma react to the news of the stuck bus?
>They were glad to see justice done, though they did not know that their children were responsible.

4. Who were the "riders," and what were they doing?
>They were a gang of white men who rode in a convoy of cars out to the black neighborhoods to burn and hurt the black people who had supposedly stepped out of their "proper" place.

Chapter 4

1. Why was Cassie upset?
>She thought the night men were after her and the boys for digging out the hole in the road and causing the white school bus to break down.

2. Why were the night men actually out the night Cassie saw them?
>They had come to tar and feather Mr. Tatum for calling Mr. Barnett a liar.

3. Why had Papa hired Mr. Morrison?
>He knew that there was racial trouble in the area, and he wanted Mr. Morrison to be at his home to protect his family while he was out working on the railroad.

4. Why did Stacey get whipped?
   His mother, the teacher, thought that he had been cheating on a test. Instead of explaining that T.J. was the cheater and had slipped the notes to him to get rid of them, Stacey accepted the punishment which should have been for T.J.

5. What did Mama do when she found out that the children had been at the Wallaces' store?
   Her immediate reaction was relatively calm. On Saturday, however, she took the children to see Mr. Berry, whom the Wallaces had burned. She wanted the children to see what kind of people the Wallaces were and the cruelty of which they were capable.

6. Why did Mama try to convince Mr. Turner to stop shopping at the Wallaces' store?
   She was trying to organize a boycott of the store in protest of the burnings.

Chapter 5

1. Why was Cassie disappointed in Strawberry?
   She had expected Strawberry to be a big, bustling city. Instead, it was a sad, red place with hardly anything modern.

2. Why did Big Ma park her wagon away from the entrance?
   The spaces closest to the entrance were reserved for white people's wagons.

3. Why did Cassie like Mr. Jamison?
   He was the only white man who had ever called Big Ma "missus," and he always answered her questions in a direct manner.

4. What made Cassie yell at Mr. Barnett?
   Cassie resented the fact that Mr. Barnett waited on the white customers before he waited on her. She understood that perhaps adults should be waited on before her since she was a child, but when Mr. Barnett waited on a white girl, that was the last straw.

Chapter 6

1. Why was Cassie mad at Big Ma?
   Cassie was mad because Big Ma had taken Mr. Simms' side in the sidewalk incident in Strawberry. Cassie did not think that she owed Lillian Jean any more of an apology than she had already given, but Mr. Simms insisted on one. When Big Ma came, she made Cassie apologize. Cassie didn't realize that Big Ma only did what she had to do to prevent anyone from being even more hurt.

2. Identify Uncle Hammer.
   Hammer was David Logan's brother, Big Ma's only other living son. He came to visit the Logans. He had a quick temper and didn't believe in waiting for diplomatic solutions to problems. He was a kind, generous, though somewhat aloof, person.

3. What explanation did Mama give Cassie for Mr. Simms' actions?
>Mama told Cassie that Mr. Simms was one of those people who didn't have much in his life, so he had to put other people down so he could feel more important himself.

4. What happened to Stacey's new coat? What was Uncle Hammer's reaction?
>T.J. made fun of Stacey's new coat until Stacey gave it to him. Uncle Hammer told Stacey that T.J. could keep the coat; if Stacey was fool enough to let someone talk him out of having it, he didn't deserve to have it.

5. How did Uncle Hammer and the Logans surprise the Wallaces?
>Usually black people were supposed to back up and let the white people cross first, but because Hammer's car looked just like Mr. Granger's, the Wallaces assumed that Mr. Granger was coming across, and they waited. The Wallaces were quite surprised to see Hammer Logan tipping his hat to them as he went by.

Chapter 7

1. Why were the last few days of school before Christmas difficult for Cassie?
>She missed her Papa, Lillian Jean was flaunting her victory, and T.J. was flaunting Stacey's coat.

2. Why didn't Papa want to back people's credit with his land?
>If the people couldn't pay their bills, he would have to sell his land to pay the bills he guaranteed.

3. What did Jeremy give Stacey?
>He gave Stacey a hand-made flute.

4. What papers did Big Ma sign?
>She signed papers which gave title of the land to Papa and Uncle Hammer, so that when she would die, there would be no question about the ownership of the land.

5. Why did Mr. Jamison want to back the people's credit?
>He felt that the Wallaces were wrong, and he wanted to help the boycott effort. Since he did no shopping there himself, the best he could do would be to put up the money to back other people's credit.

6. What did Mr. Granger say to the Logans?
>He said that because of the Logans, the peace of the community was being shattered, and he didn't like it. He said that if the Logans didn't stop the boycott, he would do whatever it would take to stop it himself and that he'd also do whatever it would take to get the Logan land back.

Chapter 8

1. What was Cassie doing for Lillian Jean?
    She was being her "slave" friend in order to get close to Lillian Jean as a part of her plan for revenge.

2. Why did Cassie take Lillian Jean into the woods?
    No one could see them there from the road. Cassie wanted no witnesses to see that she and Lillian Jean were fighting. As revenge for the Strawberry incident, Cassie had become friends with Lillian Jean. Lillian Jean divulged private information about herself and her friends to Cassie. Armed with that knowledge, Cassie was free to take Lillian Jean into the woods and give her a good punch without fear of reprisals.

3. Why did Mama lose her teaching job?
    She was fired because she was teaching things that were not in the history books but also because she was stirring up trouble with the boycott.

4. Who sicced the school board on Mama?
    T.J. did.

5. What was T.J.'s punishment?
    Everyone at school shunned him for causing Mrs. Logan to lose her job.

Chapter 9

1. What were R.W. and Melvin doing to T.J.?
    They were pretending to be his friends and then laughing at him behind his back.

2. Why were Mr. Avery and Mr. Lanier not going to shop in Vicksburg anymore?
    The Wallaces, Grangers and Montiers were threatening to take a larger portion of their crops if they would continue the boycott. The tenant farmers couldn't afford to lose any more of their crops; they needed the money to live.

3. Why were Mr. Morrison, Papa and Stacey late coming home?
    Someone had tampered with the wheels of their wagon, which came off. While trying to repair the wagon, David was shot, the horses bolted, and the wagon fell on David, breaking his leg.

4. Who shot Papa and tried to kill Mr. Morrison?
    The Wallaces were responsible.

Chapter 10

1. Why didn't Papa want to borrow money from Hammer?
    If Hammer would have found out that Papa was home instead of working on the railroad, his temper would have flared, and there could be even more trouble for the Logans.

2. How did Mr. Morrison avoid Kaleb Wallace?
> He simply picked up Kaleb's car and moved it. Later he said he wasn't very afraid because men like Kaleb don't act alone, they only act when they are in a group.

3. Why did the Logans finally have to depend on Uncle Hammer for money?
> The bank called their note due.

4. Where did Hammer get the money for the mortgage?
> He sold his car and a few other of his possessions.

5. How had T.J. changed?
> He wore fancy clothes and was very condescending. But, beneath it all, he was even lonelier than ever.

Chapter 11

1. What happened to T.J.?
> He was beaten up by the Simms brothers because he threatened to tell that they were the ones who had broken into the Barnetts' store.

2. Why did Stacey send Cassie and her brothers home?
> Cassie was supposed to go for help since the situation at the Avery house was getting out of hand. Stacey didn't think Mr. Jamison could fight off the mob for much longer, and the mob was threatening a lynching.

Chapter 12

1. What stopped the mob?
> There was a fire in the cotton field threatening to spread into the woods. If the woods had caught on fire, the whole area and everyone's crops could have been ruined. Everyone worked together to put out the fire and temporarily forgot about the lynchings.

2. How did the fire start?
> Everyone thought that lightning had started the fire, but David Logan had started it as a diversion to stop the mob.

3. What happened to T.J.?
> The sheriff took him to jail where he would be safe from the mob. It is implied that T.J. would be convicted of breaking into the Barnetts' store and hurting them.

4. Why did Cassie cry?
> She cried about the events of the evening, for T.J. and for the land.

MULTIPLE CHOICE STUDY GUIDE/QUIZ QUESTIONS - *Roll of Thunder, Hear My Cry*

Chapter 1
1. Why was Little Man lagging behind?
    A. He was afraid to go to school for the first time.
    B. He was studying the plants and insects along the road.
    C. He was being careful not to get his clothes dirty.
    D. He had a sore foot and couldn't walk as fast as the others.

2. Why was Stacey in a bad mood?
    A. He was repeating the seventh grade.
    B. He didn't like being in charge of walking the younger children to school.
    C. He hated school because he still could not read.
    D. His mother was his teacher, and he didn't want to be in her class.

3. What made Papa need to find work?
    A. He was no longer strong enough to do the farming.
    B. The price of cotton had dropped, and money was short.
    C. He wanted to get away from the noise of the children.
    D. He needed extra money to take the family to visit his brother.

4. What happened to the Berrys?
    A. They were burned when a white man set fire to them.
    B. They lost most of their crop to insects.
    C. They were drowned while trying to cross the river.
    D. The owner of their land evicted them.

5. How did T. J. get out of his punishment?
    A. He told his mother he had been studying with Stacey.
    B. He cried and promised he would be better from then on.
    C. He told his mother that he had gone to the Wallaces' store to get his brother Claude.
    D. He talked his father into taking his side against his mother.

6. Who was Jeremy?
    A. A black neighbor and friend of the Logan children
    B. A rich white boy who taunted the Logans
    C. A black orphan who lived with the Logans
    D. A shy white boy who liked to walk to school with the Logans

Roll of Thunder Multiple Choice Study Questions Page 2

7. Which of these statements describes Cassie?
    A. She is a fourth grade student who despises dressing up and sticks up for her own rights.
    B. She is a seventh grade student who is very belligerent and is in constant conflict with her parents and teachers.
    C. She is a fifth grade student who is very shy and rarely speaks to anyone.
    D. She is a first grade student who is bright and learned to read at an early age.

8. What was new and exciting about this school year?
    A. The black students would go to school as long as the white students.
    B. This was the first year the black students had books other than the Bible.
    C. The black and white students would be going to the same school.
    D. The black students would have their own bus.

9. Why did Cassie and Little Man refuse to take their readers?
    A. In the front of the books, the black students were called "nigra." The books were handed down from the white school and were in poor condition.
    B. They had both seen dead bugs inside the readers and were afraid of finding more.
    C. They were embarrassed to admit that they could not read.
    D. They were afraid Big Ma would whip them for reading anything but the Bible.

10. How did Mary Logan react to Daisy's news about the children's refusal to accept the books?
    A. She beat them both for being disrespectful to a teacher.
    B. She yelled at Daisy for daring to hit her children.
    C. She politely dismissed Daisy's anger because she understood her children.
    D. She cried and begged Daisy not to tell the principal.

Roll of Thunder Multiple Choice Study Questions Page 3

<u>Chapter 2</u>

11. Describe Mr. Morrison. Why did Papa hire him?
    - A. He was a short, nervous man for whom Papa felt sorry.
    - B. He was tall and intellectual. Papa had hired him to tutor the children.
    - C. He was of average height and rather heavy. Papa hired him to build an extra room on the house.
    - D. He was tall and formidable. Papa hired him as a farm hand.

12. What did Mr. Morrison tell the Logans about his past?
    - A. He had never been to school.
    - B. He had been in trouble for beating up a white man.
    - C. His wife and children had left him and moved to New York.
    - D. He used to be a drunkard, but now he had stopped drinking.

13. How did the congregation feel about the burnings?
    - A. They were glad the people got what they deserved.
    - B. They were upset but felt the law was taking care of things properly.
    - C. They were angry and made a plan to attack the whites.
    - D. They were disgusted and felt that not enough was being done about it.

14. Why didn't Papa want the children to go to the Wallaces' store?
    - A. People went there to drink and carouse, and the children usually ended up in trouble. It wasn't a wholesome place for children.
    - B. Papa thought that music and dancing were sinful. He did not want his children to associate with sinners.
    - C. The store was a long way from home. He didn't want them to walk that far.
    - D. He was afraid the children would act up and embarrass him.

Roll of Thunder Multiple Choice Study Questions Page 4

Chapter 3
15. What was the problem with the Jefferson Davis school bus?
    A. It was old and broke down at least once a week, and the white students didn't want to walk to school with the black students.
    B. The new driver was black. Some of the white students refused to ride without a white driver..
    C. The driver would run the black children off the road so the white children could jeer at them.
    D. It was supposed to pick up the black students, but the driver didn't always stop.

16. Why did the Logan children dig a hole in the road?
    A. They thought it would help drain the water away from the bank.
    B. They wanted to get even with the bus driver and kids by causing the bus to get stuck.
    C. They thought the road would flood and then they would not have to go to school for a few days.
    D. T.J. had offered them money to do it. He wanted Mr.Granger's car to get muddy.

17. How did Mama and Big Ma react to the news of the stuck bus?
    A. They were upset and went to help get the bus out of the hole.
    B. They were afraid there would be a flood if the rain had already washed out part of the road.
    C. They were not interested because they said it was white people's business.
    D. They were glad to see justice done, although they did not know that their children were responsible.

18. Who were the "riders," and what were they doing?
    A. They were the white students who were brought to school by horse and wagon while the bus was being repaired.
    B. They were a gang of white men who rode in a convoy of cars out to the black neighborhoods to burn and hurt the black people who had supposedly stepped out of their place.
    C. They were a group of black men who rode through the area on horseback delivering mail and supplies to people in the area.
    D. They were the railroad bosses who rode over the newly laid track to inspect it. If they didn't like it, the workers didn't get paid.

Roll of Thunder Multiple Choice Study Questions Page 5

Chapter 4
19. Why was Cassie upset?
    A. She thought the night men were after her and her brothers for digging the hole.
    B. She had broken the best butter dish and was afraid her mother would beat her.
    C. She felt sick and thought she had caught the flu while digging the hole.
    D. She wanted to go out and play, but her mother was making her stay inside and churn the butter.

20. Why were the night men actually out the night Cassie saw them?
    A. They were coming out to steal tools from the barn.
    B. They were going to a meeting at Mr. Granger's house and got lost.
    C. They had come to tar and feather Mr. Tatum for calling Mr. Barnett a liar.
    D. They were trying to scare the black families into telling who had damaged the road.

21. Why had Papa hired Mr. Morrison?
    A. He wanted Mr. Morrison to protect his family while he was away.
    B. He owed Mr. Morrison a favor from the last job they worked together.
    C. Papa felt sorry because Mr. Morrison had no family.
    D. He wanted to embarrass Stacey into acting more like a man.

22. Why did Stacey get whipped?
    A. He tore the brown paper off the inside of the text book and refused to use it.
    B. He started a fight with two white boys who were walking by the schoolyard.
    C. He refused to do any work in his mother's room and got the other students to also stop working.
    D. He was taking the punishment for T.J.'s cheating, since he wouldn't tell on T.J.

23. What did Mama do when she found out that the children had been at the Wallaces' store?
    A. She whipped them and sent them to their rooms.
    B. She took them to see Mr. Berry, who had been burned by the Wallaces.
    C. She cried and told them how hard it was for her when her husband was gone.
    D. She said she would not help them if they got into trouble at the store.

24. Why did Mama try to convince Mr. Turner to stop shopping at the Wallaces' store?
    A. She wanted him to shop around for lower prices.
    B. She thought he was spending too much money and should save some.
    C. She was trying to organize a boycott of the store to protest the burnings.
    D. She wanted him to give money to the church instead.

Roll of Thunder Multiple Choice Study Questions Page 6

Chapter 5

25. Why was Cassie disappointed in Strawberry?
    A. She had expected Strawberry to be a bigger, more modern city than it was.
    B. She thought there would be plenty of strawberry dishes to eat, and that was her favorite fruit.
    C. It was crowded and noisy. She liked wide open spaces.
    D. Big Ma didn't let her do anything but sit in the wagon.

26. Why did Big Ma park her wagon away from the entrance?
    A. She was shy, and the crowds scared her.
    B. Her wagon was bigger than the others and would only fit in the back.
    C. She got there late, and the spaces up front were all full.
    D. The front spaces were reserved for the white people.

27. Why did Cassie like Mr. Jamison?
    A. She liked looking at his fancy clothes and car.
    B. He was the only white man who had ever called Big Ma "missus," and he always answered her questions directly.
    C. He had saved her from drowning when she was small.
    D. He had donated books to the black school and was trying to help them get a school bus.

28. What made Cassie yell at Mr. Barnett?
    A. She could see that a sack of flour was going to fall off the shelf onto his head, and she wanted him to get out of the way.
    B. She was angry that he waited on a white child who had come in the store after them..
    C. He said he would only sell candy to white children.
    D. She didn't think he should have guns on display in the front counter.

Roll of Thunder Multiple Choice Study Questions Page 7

Chapter 6

29. Why was Cassie mad at Big Ma?
    A. Big Ma refused to buy her candy or pretty hair ribbons.
    B. She wanted to drive the wagon home and Big Ma said no.
    C. Big Ma made her apologize to Lillian Jean.
    D. Big Ma would not let her visit with Mr. Jamison and his family.

30. Which of these phrases does not describe Uncle Hammer?
    A. Owns a carpentry business
    B. Quick temper
    C. Lives in the North
    D. Kind, generous, sometimes aloof

31. What explanation did Mama give Cassie for Mr. Simms' actions?
    A. Mr. Simms was losing his mind and didn't realize what he did or said.
    B. Mr. Simms had mistaken her for another girl who had hurt his daughter.
    C. Mr. Simms never went to church, so he didn't know Christian behavior.
    D. Mr. Simms had to put others down so he could feel important himself.

32. What happened to Stacey's new coat? What was Uncle Hammer's reaction?
    A. Stacey got it dirty the first time he wore it. Uncle Hammer said not to worry and helped Stacey clean it up.
    B. T. J. talked Stacey into giving him the coat. Uncle Hammer said if Stacey were fool enough to get talked out of it, then T. J. should keep it.
    C. Stacey hid the coat in his closet because he didn't like it. Uncle Hammer said he would never buy Stacey another present.
    D. It shrank in the rain. Uncle Hammer said he would return it to the store.

33. How did Uncle Hammer and the Logans surprise the Wallaces?
    A. They all went to the Wallaces' store to listen to music.
    B. They smiled and were friendly even though the Wallaces were rude.
    C. The Wallaces thought they were letting the Grangers' car cross the bridge first, but it was really Uncle Hammer.
    D. Uncle Hammer and Papa offered to buy the Wallaces' store.

Roll of Thunder Multiple Choice Study Questions Page 8

<u>Chapter 7</u>

34. Why were the last few days of school before Christmas difficult for Cassie?
    A. She missed her Papa, Lillian Jean was flaunting her victory, and T. J. was flaunting Stacey's coat.
    B. She had a lead part in the Christmas show and was having trouble remembering her lines.
    C. Uncle Hammer had put wrapped boxes in the living room. Cassie was curious to know what was in them.
    D. It was cold, and she didn't like wearing her shoes. She was also upset because she was trying to make gifts for her family and didn't have enough time alone to work on them.

35. Why didn't Papa want to back people's credit with his land?
    A. He didn't really like his neighbors enough to do that for them.
    B. If the people couldn't pay their bills, he would have to sell his land for the bills he guaranteed.
    C. Mama said she would not speak to him if he did it.
    D. He was afraid of what the white men might do to him.

36. What did Jeremy give Stacey?
    A. A hand-made flute
    B. A hard-backed book
    C. A young hunting dog
    D. Some of his old clothes

37. What papers did Big Ma sign?
    A. An agreement to back the neighbors' credit
    B. A formal complaint against Mr. Simms for hurting Cassie
    C. A title transfer to give the land to Papa and Uncle Hammer
    D. A contract donating part of her forest to the church

38. Why did Mr. Jamison want to back the people's credit?
    A. He was co-owner of the store in Vicksburg and wanted to drive the Wallaces out of business.
    B. He knew they couldn't pay, and then he could get their land.
    C. He wanted to get more business from the black community.
    D. He felt the Wallaces were wrong and wanted to help the boycott.

Roll of Thunder Multiple Choice Study Questions Page 9

39. What did Mr. Granger say to the Logans?
    A. No black in town could have a car as nice as his, and Uncle Hammer would have to leave immediately.
    B. The Logans were shattering the peace of the community. He would do whatever he had to to stop the boycott and get the Logans' land.
    C. He was glad the blacks were standing up to the Wallaces. He would donate a wagon to use for the trips to Vicksburg.
    D. They were being unreasonable. He would go with them to talk to the Wallaces and straighten things out.

Roll of Thunder Multiple Choice Study Questions Page 10

Chapter 8

40. What was Cassie doing for Lillian Jean, and why?
    A. Cassie was being her "slave friend" in order to get close to Lillian Jean as part of her plan for revenge.
    B. Cassie was being especially kind to her because her (Cassie's) Papa said she had to or she would be punished at home.
    C. Cassie thought if she could get Lillian Jean to play with her, then none of her white friends would play with her. If Lillian Jean didn't have any other friends, then she would be nice to Cassie.
    D. Cassie wanted to understand white people better. She was trying to do that by getting close to Lillian Jean.

41. Why did Cassie take Lillian Jean into the woods?
    A. There were some beautiful wildflowers that Cassie knew Lillian Jean would like to see.
    B. Cassie planned to get Lillian Jean lost and then leave her there to scare her.
    C. Cassie didn't want any witnesses to see that she and Lillian Jean were fighting.
    D. Cassie had built a secret tree house that she wanted to show to Lillian Jean.

42. Why did Mama lose her teaching job?
    A. There weren't enough students in the seventh grade, so the principal had to fire one teacher and put the students in another class.
    B. The school board didn't think she should be teaching in the same school that her children attended.
    C. She was not supposed to whip the students, but she did it anyway.
    D. She was not teaching what was in the history books, and she was stirring up trouble with the boycott.

43. Who told the school board on Mama?
    A. Lillian Jean
    B. T.J.
    C. Mr. Wellever
    D. Mrs. Crocker

44. What was T.J.'s punishment?
    A. Mr. Avery whipped him and made him apologize.
    B. He was expelled from school.
    C. He had to go and sit in the first grade classroom for a week.
    D. Everyone at school shunned (ignored) him.

Roll of Thunder Multiple Choice Study Questions Page 11

Chapter 9

45. What were R. W. and Melvin doing to T.J., and why?
    A. They were being kind, hoping that some of the other white children would follow their example.
    B. They were making friends just to disobey and anger their father.
    C. They were pretending to be his friends and then laughing behind his back.
    D. They were using him to convince the others to start shopping at the Wallaces' store again.

46. Why were Mr. Avery and Mr. Lanier going to stop shopping in Vicksburg?
    A. The white landowners were threatening to take a larger share of the tenant farmers' crops if the boycott continued.
    B. They didn't like the prices or the quality of the supplies from Vicksburg.
    C. The person who was backing their credit stopped doing it, and they couldn't afford to go there anymore.
    D. The supplies from Vicksburg didn't come often enough. They liked the convenience of the Wallaces' store better.

47. Why were Mr. Morrison, Papa, and Stacey late coming home?
    A. They stopped and had dinner with Mr. Jamison. They had such a good time talking that they didn't realize how late it was.
    B. Papa and Mr. Morrison fell asleep in the back of the wagon. Stacey was driving and took the wrong road. They had to retrace their steps to get back on the correct road.
    C. Someone had tampered with the wagon wheels. While they were fixing them, David was shot. The horses bolted, and the wagon fell on David.
    D. When they were halfway home, they realized they had forgotten to get some of the things on Mama's list. They went back to pick up the items.

48. Who shot Papa and tried to kill Mr. Morrison?
    A. T.J., R.W., and Melvin
    B. Mr. Avery and Mr. Lanier
    C. The Wallaces
    D. Mr. Granger and Mr. Montier

Roll of Thunder Multiple Choice Study Questions Page 12

Chapter 10

49. Why didn't Papa want to borrow money from Hammer?
    A. Papa was embarrassed to let Hammer know that he could not take proper care of his family.
    B. If Papa borrowed money and couldn't repay it, then the land would all go to Hammer. Papa and his family would have to move.
    C. Papa knew Hammer didn't have very much himself and didn't want to be a bother.
    D. If Hammer knew that Papa was home instead of working on the railroad, his temper could have flared and there could have been more trouble.

50. How did Mr. Morrison avoid Kaleb Wallace?
    A. He picked up Kaleb's car and moved it out of the way.
    B. He took another road instead.
    C. He sat and waited and pretended to be asleep.
    D. He stayed home and sent Stacey on the errand.

51. Why did the Logans finally have to depend on Uncle Hammer for money?
    A. Papa found out he could never work again.
    B. The bank called their note due.
    C. Mr. Granger was selling some land, and they wanted to buy it.
    D. Big Ma convinced them it was the best thing to do.

52. Where did Uncle Hammer get the money for the mortgage?
    A. He sold his car and a few other things and borrowed some of it.
    B. He worked overtime at his job.
    C. He had a very large bank account.
    D. The congregation at his church donated it.

53. How had T.J. changed?
    A. He had started studying and passed all of his tests.
    B. He got religion and gave up his association with Melvin and R.W.
    C. He was getting violent. Even Melvin and R.W. were afraid of him.
    D. He wore fancy clothes and was very condescending.

Roll of Thunder Multiple Choice Study Questions Page 13

Chapter 11
54. What happened to T.J.?
- A. He got a scholarship to go to school and study to be a minister.
- B. He got very sick and couldn't get out of bed for a month.
- C. He was beaten up by the Simms brothers when he threatened to tell on them.
- D. He was expelled from school, and his father kicked him out of the house.

55. Why did Stacey send Cassie and her brothers home?
- A. He wanted her to steal Papa's gun and bring it back to him.
- B. He sent her to go for help because the situation was getting worse.
- C. It was after their bedtime, and he didn't want to get into trouble for keeping them out late.
- D. They were making too much noise, and he was afraid they would be discovered.

Chapter 12
56. What stopped the mob?
    A. Mr. Jamison finally convinced them he was right.
    B. They all went to fight the fire in the cotton field.
    C. The sheriff and his deputies threatened to arrest them all.
    D. The Simms boys told the truth.

57. How did the fire really start?
    A. The Wallaces set it.
    B. Lightning struck the cotton.
    C. Little Man and Christopher-John were playing with matches.
    D. David Logan set it as a diversion to stop the mob.

58. What happened to T.J.?
    A. He was severely burned trying to fight the fire.
    B. He was rushed to the hospital in Vicksburg.
    C. The sheriff took him to jail.
    D. He died from his stomach wounds.

59. Why did Cassie cry?
    A. She was upset about the events of the evening, T.J, and the land.
    B. She wanted to help fight the fire and was not allowed to.
    C. She was sad that she would never ride in Uncle Hammer's car again.
    D. She thought Papa, Stacey, and Mr. Morrison had been killed in the fire.

ANSWER KEY - MULTIPLE CHOICE STUDY/QUIZ QUESTIONS
Roll of Thunder, Hear My Cry

Chapters 1-2	Chapters 3-4	Chapters 5-6	Chapters 7-8	Chapters 9-10	Chapters 11-12
1. C	15. C	25. A	34. A	45. C	54. C
2. D	16. B	26. D	35. B	46. A	55. B
3. B	17. D	27. B	36. A	47. C	56. B
4. A	18. B	28. B	37. C	48. C	57. D
5. C	19. A	29. C	38. D	49. D	58. C
6. D	20. C	30. A	39. B	50. A	59. A
7. A	21. A	31. D	40. A	51. B	
8. B	22. D	32. B	41. C	52. A	
9. A	23. B	33. C	42. D	53. D	
10. C	24. C		43. B		
11. D			44. D		
12. B					
13. D					
14. A					

PREREADING VOCABULARY WORKSHEETS

VOCABULARY - *Roll of Thunder, Hear My Cry*

Chapters 1-2 Part I: Using Prior Knowledge and Contextual Clues

Below are the sentences in which the vocabulary words above appear in the text. Read the sentence. Use any clues you can find in the sentence combined with your prior knowledge, and write what you think the underlined words mean on the lines provided.

1. It seemed to me that showing up at school at all on a bright August-like October morning . . . was <u>concession</u> enough; Sunday clothing was asking too much.

   _____

2. "Ah, Cassie, leave him be," Stacey <u>admonished</u>, frowning and kicking testily at the road.

   _____

3. "Ain't no need gettin' mad," T.J. replied <u>undaunted</u>. "How you know?" I questioned <u>suspiciously</u>.

   _____

4. Stacey pulled back, considering whether or not T.J.'s words were offensive, but T.J. immediately erased the question by continuing <u>amiably</u>.

   _____

5. He was often <u>ridiculed</u> by the other children at his school and had shown up more than once with wide red welts on his arms which Lillian Jean, his older sister, had revealed with satisfaction were the result of his associating with us.

   _____

6. In front of it were two yellow buses, our own tormentor and one that brought students from the other direction, and <u>loitering</u> students awaiting the knell of the morning bell.

   _____

7. He just stood staring down at the open book, shivering with <u>indignant</u> anger.

   _____

8. I glanced at the boys and it was <u>obvious</u> to me that they were wondering the same thing as I....

   _____

Vocabulary - *Roll of Thunder, Hear My Cry* Chapters 1-2 Continued

Part II: Determining the Meaning

You have tried to figure out the meanings of the vocabulary words for Chapter 1. Now match the vocabulary words to their dictionary definitions. If there are words for which you cannot figure out the definition by contextual clues and by process of elimination, look them up in a dictionary.

___ 1. undaunted   A. hanging around with nothing particular to do
___ 2. amiably   B. a compromise
___ 3. ridiculed   C. easy to see or understand
___ 4. loitering   D. made someone the object of scornful laughter
___ 5. indignant   E. not faltering or hesitating
___ 6. concession   F. feeling anger at something unjust
___ 7. admonished   G. cautioned against; warned
___ 8. obvious   H. having a pleasant and friendly disposition

Vocabulary - *Roll of Thunder, Hear My Cry* Chapters 3-4

Part I: Using Prior Knowledge and Contextual Clues

Below are the sentences in which the vocabulary words above appear in the text. Read the sentence. Use any clues you can find in the sentence combined with your prior knowledge, and write what you think the underlined words mean on the lines provided.

1. Knowing that the bus driver liked to entertain his passengers by sending us slipping along the road to the almost <u>inaccessible</u> forest banks . . . we continuously looked over our shoulders. . .

_____

2. It was as if the bus were a living thing, <u>plaguing</u> and defeated us at every turn.

_____

3. And for once in his life, Little man was happily <u>oblivious</u> to the mud spattering upon him.

_____

4. John and Christopher-John nudged Little Man, and the three of us forced ourselves to stare into the fire in <u>feigned</u> disinterest.

_____

5. I had learned that at times like these it was better to just sit and wait than to go asking disrupting questions with might <u>vex</u> her.

_____

6. Yet just one glance at each other and we were lost, slumping on the table in helpless, <u>contagious</u> laughter.

_____

7. I crept <u>precariously</u> near the edge of the high porch. . . .

_____

8. She also spoke of finding another store to <u>patronize</u>, one where the proprietors were more concerned about the welfare of the community.

_____

Vocabulary - *Roll of Thunder, Hear My Cry* Chapters 3-4

Part II: Determining the Meaning

You have tried to figure out the meanings of the vocabulary words for Chapter 2 & 3. Now match the vocabulary words to their dictionary definitions. If there are words for which you cannot figure out the definition by contextual clues and by process of elimination, look them up in a dictionary.

___ 9. inaccessible
___ 10. plaguing
___ 11. oblivious
___ 12. contagiously
___ 13. precariously
___ 14. patronize
___ 15. vex
___ 16. feigned

A. unaware of; not mindful of
B. dangerously lacking in stability or security
C. impossible to reach or enter
D. pretended
E. afflicting; troubling
F. to trouble or bother
G. easily transmitted; catching
H. to go to regularly as a customer

Vocabulary - *Roll of Thunder, Hear My Cry* Chapter 5-6

Part I: Using Prior Knowledge and Contextual Clues
    Below are the sentences in which the vocabulary words above appear in the text. Read the sentence. Use any clues you can find in the sentence combined with your prior knowledge, and write what you think the underlined words mean on the lines provided.

1. "I already know what I am!" I retaliated.

_____

2. His eyes, which showed a great warmth as he hugged and kissed us now, often had a cold, distant glaze, and there was an aloofness in him which the boys and I could never quite bridge.

_____

3. Big Ma nodded mutely and I went on.

_____

4. Suddenly Mama lunged to the side door, blocking it with her slender body.

_____

5. "If he don't" said Little Man ominously, "I betcha Uncle Hammer'll teach that ole Mr. Simms a thing or two.

_____

6. "I ain't nobody's little nigger!" I screamed, angry and humiliated.

_____

7. I watched him go, but did not follow. Instead, I ambled along the sidewalk trying to understand why Mr. Barnett had acted the way he had.

_____

Vocabulary - *Roll of Thunder, Hear My Cry* Chapters 5-6 Continued

Part II: Determining the Meaning

You have tried to figure out the meanings of the vocabulary words for Chapters 5 & 6. Now match the vocabulary words to their dictionary definitions. If there are words for which you cannot figure out the definition by contextual clues and by process of elimination, look them up in a dictionary.

___ 17. ambled   A. returned like for like
___ 18. retaliated   B. threateningly
___ 19. humiliated   C. at a distance; removed
___ 20. ominously   D. without speaking
___ 21. lunged   E. suddenly thrust
___ 22. aloofness   F. lowered in pride or dignity
___ 23. mutely   G. moved at a smooth, easy gait

Vocabulary - *Roll of Thunder, Hear My Cry* Chapters 7-8

Part I: Using Prior Knowledge and Contextual Clues

Below are the sentences in which the vocabulary words above appear in the text. Read the sentence. Use any clues you can find in the sentence combined with your prior knowledge, and write what you think the underlined words mean on the lines provided.

1. Christopher-John, Little Man, and I exchanged apprehensive glances.

_____

2. The last days of school before Christmas seemed interminable.

_____

3. Mr. Jamison nodded. He was a long, thin man in his mid-fifties with a perfect lawyer face, so placid that it was difficult to guess what thoughts lay behind it.

_____

4. You back the credit with it now and he'll seize this opportunity to take it away from you.

_____

5. "Mama gonna whip you good, too," said prideful Little Man, still fuming as we approached the school.

_____

6. When we caught up with them, it was obvious that the jovial mask T.J. always wore had been stripped away.

_____

7. Avoiding us in the morning, he arrived late, only to be shunned by the other students.

_____

8. I don't think your Paul Edward would've condoned something like this and risked losing this place.

_____

Vocabulary - *Roll of Thunder, Hear My Cry* Chapters 7-8 Continued

Part II: Determining the Meaning
You have tried to figure out the meanings of the vocabulary words for Chapter 7 & 8. Now match the vocabulary words to their dictionary definitions. If there are words for which you cannot figure out the definition by contextual clues and by process of elimination, look them up in a dictionary.

___ 24. condoned
___ 25. seize
___ 26. placid
___ 27. apprehensive
___ 28. interminable
___ 29. jovial
___ 30. shunned
___ 31. fuming

A. tranquil; calm
B. full of hearty, playful good humor
C. boiling over with anger
D. endorsed; given his blessings for
E. ignored; kept out of association
F. to grasp; take; arrest
G. unending
H. anxious; uneasy

Vocabulary - *Roll of Thunder, Hear My Cry* Chapter 9-10

Part I: Using Prior Knowledge and Contextual Clues

    Below are the sentences in which the vocabulary words above appear in the text. Read the sentence. Use any clues you can find in the sentence combined with your prior knowledge, and write what you think the underlined words mean on the lines provided.

1. A few minutes later he <u>emerged</u> from the field alone, got into his car, and left.

_____

2. Mama laughed lightly in <u>exasperation</u>.

_____

3. Christopher-John, Little Man, and I stared open-mouthed and even Stacey, who had witnessed Mr. Morrison's <u>phenomenal</u> strength before, gazed in wonder.

_____

4. The heat swooped low over the land clinging like an invisible <u>shroud</u> and through it people moved slowly lethargically, as if under water.

_____

5. Long hours after we should have been in bed, we sat on the front porch lit only by the whiteness of the full moon and listened to the comforting sounds of Papa's and Uncle Hammer's voices <u>mingling</u> once again.

_____

6. "No," said Papa <u>adamantly</u>, "you do better in Chicago."

_____

7. Melvin nodded, a <u>condescending</u> smirk on his face which was lost on T.J.

_____

Vocabulary - *Roll of Thunder, Hear My Cry* Chapters 9-10 Continued

Part II: Determining the Meaning

    You have tried to figure out the meanings of the vocabulary words for Chapters 9 & 10. Now match the vocabulary words to their dictionary definitions. If there are words for which you cannot figure out the definition by contextual clues and by process of elimination, look them up in a dictionary.

___ 32. emerged   A. extremely unusual
___ 33. exasperation   B. boldly; not giving in; firmly
___ 34. shroud   C. something that conceals or screens like a garment
___ 35. phenomenal   D. descending voluntarily to the level of an inferior person
___ 36. condescending   E. mixing together
___ 37. adamantly   F. came forth into view
___ 38. mingling   G. irritation or annoyance

Vocabulary - *Roll of Thunder, Hear My Cry* Chapter 11-12

Part I: Using Prior Knowledge and Contextual Clues

    Below are the sentences in which the vocabulary words above appear in the text. Read the sentence. Use any clues you can find in the sentence combined with your prior knowledge, and write what you think the underlined words mean on the lines provided.

1. A <u>crescendo</u> of ugly hate rose from the men as the second car approached.

_____

2. Afterward both Mama and Big Ma changed their clothes, then we sat, very quiet, as the heat crept sticky and wet through our clothing and the thunder banged <u>menacingly</u> overhead.

_____

3. "Hush, Cassie," Stacey said, his eyes <u>intent</u> on the men.

_____

4. Perhaps he felt that even a person as despicable as T.J. needed someone he could call "friend," or perhaps he sensed T.J.'s <u>vulnerability</u> better than T.J. did himself.

_____

Part II: Determining the Meaning

    You have tried to figure out the meanings of the vocabulary words for Chapters 10-12. Now match the vocabulary words to their dictionary definitions. If there are words for which you cannot figure out the definition by contextual clues and by process of elimination, look them up in a dictionary.

___ 39. intent   A. threateningly
___ 40. menacingly   B. a gradual increase in loudness or intensity
___ 41. crescendo   C. concentrating on a single purpose; engrossed
___ 42. vulnerability   D. ability to be injured or wounded

ANSWER KEY - VOCABULARY
Roll of Thunder, Hear My Cry

Chapters 1-2	Chapters 3-4	Chapters 5-6
1. E	9. C	17. G
2. H	10. E	18. A
3. D	11. A	19. F
4. A	12. G	20. B
5. F	13. B	21. E
6. B	14. H	22. C
7. G	15. F	23. D
8. C	16. D	

Chapters 7-8	Chapters 9-10	Chapters 11-12
24. D	32. F	39. C
25. F	33. G	40. A
26. A	34. C	41. B
27. H	35. A	42. D
28. G	36. D	
29. B	37. B	
30. E	38. E	
31. C		

DAILY LESSONS

LESSON ONE

Objectives
1. To introduce the *Roll of Thunder, Hear My Cry* unit
2. To distribute books and other related materials
3. To preview the study questions for chapters 1-2
4. To familiarize students with the vocabulary for chapters 1-2
5. To have students recognize the things they do in their own lives out of duty or responsibility rather than of want

Activity #1

Tell students to take out a piece of paper and to write down a list of all the things that they do because they "have to," not because they <u>want</u> to. Give students about 5 minutes to complete their lists.

Have students volunteer some of their responses from their lists. If possible, find out exactly <u>why</u> they do each of the things on their lists. Using your students' responses as a base, hold a discussion about duties and responsibilities that affect all of our lives. (You might even volunteer some things from a list of your own!)

<u>Transition:</u> Explain to students that in *Roll of Thunder, Hear My Cry* many of the characters have to put aside their own personal desires in order to do what is best, what is right, or what is their responsibility.

Activity #2

Distribute the materials students will use in this unit. Explain in detail how students are to use these materials.

<u>Study Guides</u> Students should read the study guide questions for each reading assignment prior to beginning the reading assignment to get a feeling for what events and ideas are important in the section they are about to read. After reading the section, students will (as a class or individually) answer the questions to review the important events and ideas from that section of the book. Students should keep the study guides as study materials for the unit test.

<u>Vocabulary</u> Prior to reading a reading assignment, students will do vocabulary work related to the section of the book they are about to read. Following the completion of the reading of the book, there will be a vocabulary review of all the words used in the vocabulary assignments. Students should keep their vocabulary work as study materials for the unit test.

<u>Reading Assignment Sheet</u> You need to fill in the reading assignment sheet to let students know by when their reading has to be completed. You can either write the assignment sheet up on a side blackboard or bulletin board and leave it there for students to see each day, or you can "ditto" copies for each student to have. In either case, you should advise students to become very familiar with the reading assignments so they know what is expected of them.

<u>Extra Activities Center</u> The resource sections of this unit contain suggestions for an extra library of related books and articles in your classroom as well as crossword and word search puzzles. Make an extra activities center in your room where you will keep these materials for students to use. (Bring the books and articles in from the library and keep several copies of the puzzles on hand.) Explain to students that these materials are available for students to use when they finish reading assignments or other class work early.

<u>Nonfiction Assignment Sheet</u> Explain to students that they each are to read at least one non-fiction piece from the in-class library at some time during the unit. Students will fill out a nonfiction assignment sheet after completing the reading to help you evaluate their reading experiences and to help the students think about and evaluate their own reading experiences.

<u>Books</u> Each school has its own rules and regulations regarding student use of school books. Advise students of the procedures that are normal for your school.

<u>Activity #3</u>
Preview the study questions and have students do the vocabulary work for Chapters 1-2 of *Roll of Thunder, Hear My Cry*. If students do not finish this assignment during this class period, they should complete it prior to the next class meeting.

NONFICTION ASSIGNMENT SHEET
(To be completed after reading the required nonfiction article)

Name _____ Date _____

Title of Nonfiction Read _____

Written By _____ Publication Date _____

I. Factual Summary: Write a short summary of the piece you read.

II. Vocabulary
    1. With which vocabulary words in the piece did you encounter some degree of difficulty?

    2. How did you resolve your lack of understanding with these words?

III. Interpretation: What was the main point the author wanted you to get from reading his work?

IV. Criticism
    1. With which points of the piece did you agree or find easy to accept? Why?

    2. With which points of the piece did you disagree or find difficult to believe? Why?

V. Personal Response: What do you think about this piece? <u>OR</u> How does this piece influence your ideas?

LESSON TWO

Objectives
1. To read chapters 1-2
2. To give students practice reading orally
3. To evaluate students' oral reading

Activity

Have students read chapters 1-2 of *Roll of Thunder, Hear My Cry* out loud in class. You probably know the best way to get readers with your class; pick students at random, ask for volunteers, or use whatever method works best for your group. If you have not yet completed an oral reading evaluation for your students this marking period, this would be a good opportunity to do so. A form is included with this unit for your convenience.

If students do not complete reading chapters 1-2 in class, they should do so prior to your next class meeting.

ORAL READING EVALUATION - *Roll of Thunder, Hear My Cry*

Name _____ Class____ Date _____

SKILL	EXCELLENT	GOOD	AVERAGE	FAIR	POOR
Fluency	5	4	3	2	1
Clarity	5	4	3	2	1
Audibility	5	4	3	2	1
Pronunciation	5	4	3	2	1
_____	5	4	3	2	1
_____	5	4	3	2	1

Total _____   Grade _____

Comments:

LESSON THREE

Objectives
1. To review the main events and ideas from chapters 1-2
2. To preview the study questions for chapters 3-4
3. To familiarize students with the vocabulary in chapters 3-4
4. To read chapters 3-4

Activity #1
Give students a few minutes to formulate answers for the study guide questions for chapters 1-2 and then discuss the answers to the questions in detail. Write the answers on the board or overhead transparency so students can have the correct answers for study purposes. NOTE: It is a good practice in public speaking and leadership skills for individual students to take charge of leading the discussions of the study questions. Perhaps a different student could go to the front of the class and lead the discussion each day that the study questions are discussed during this unit. Of course, the teacher should guide the discussion when appropriate and be sure to fill in any gaps the students leave.

Activity #2
Give students about fifteen minutes to preview the study questions for chapters 3-4 of *Roll of Thunder, Hear My Cry* and to do the related vocabulary work.

Activity #3
Choose students to read chapters 3-4 of *Roll of Thunder, Hear My Cry* orally during this class period. Continue and try to complete the oral reading evaluations. If students do not complete reading these chapters during the class period, they should do so prior to your next class meeting.

LESSON FOUR

Objectives
1. To review the main ideas and events from chapters 3-4
2. To preview the study questions for chapters 5-6
3. To familiarize students with the vocabulary in chapters 5-6
4. To read chapters 5-6

Activity #1

Give students a few minutes to formulate answers for the study guide questions for chapters 3-4 and then discuss the answers to the questions in detail. Write the answers on the board or overhead transparency so students can have the correct answers for study purposes.

Activity #2

Give students about 15 minutes to preview the study questions for chapters 5-6 and to do the related vocabulary work.

Activity #3

In the time that remains in the period, have students read chapters 5-6 silently. If students do not finish reading these chapters during this class period, they should do so prior to your next class meeting.

LESSON FIVE

Objectives
1. To review the main ideas and events from chapters 5-6
2. To do the prereading work for chapters 7-8
3. To read chapters 7-8
4. To give students the opportunity to practice writing to inform

Activity #1

Give students a few minutes to formulate answers for the study guide questions for chapters 5-6 and then discuss the answers to the questions in detail. Write the answers on the board or overhead transparency so students can have the correct answers for study purposes.

Activity #2

Distribute Writing Assignment #1. Discuss the directions in detail and give students ample time to complete the assignment.

Activity #3

Tell students that prior to your next class meeting they should complete the prereading and reading work for chapters 7-8.

WRITING ASSIGNMENT #1 - *Roll of Thunder, Hear My Cry*

PROMPT

You have met the Logan children and have completed reading half of the novel, *Roll of Thunder, Hear My Cry*.

Your assignment is to contrast Cassie, Stacey, Christopher-John and Little Man. Even though they are brothers and sister and have some common characteristics, they are also distinctly different people.

PREWRITING

On a piece of paper, write down the names of the four children, leaving space to write notes under each name.

Under each name write down a list of characteristics of that child.

Next to the list of characteristics, jot down at least one good example of something that character did to exemplify that trait.

DRAFTING

Begin with a paragraph in which you introduce the Logan children and explain that they do have distinct personalities.

In the body of your composition, write one paragraph about each of the children. State the main qualities of your character in the topic sentence of the paragraph and then fill in the paragraph with examples of the traits you have just said the character has.

Write a final paragraph to close your composition and to draw appropriate conclusions from the data you have provided.

PROMPT

When you finish the rough draft of your paper, ask a student who sits near you to read it. After reading your rough draft, he/she should tell you what he/she liked best about your work, which parts were difficult to understand, and ways in which your work could be improved. Reread your paper considering your critic's comments and make the corrections you think are necessary.

PROOFREADING

Do a final proofreading of your paper double-checking your grammar, spelling, organization, and the clarity of your ideas.

LESSON SIX

Objectives
1. To review the main ideas of chapters 7-8
2. To preview the study questions for chapters 9-10
3. To read chapters 9-10

Activity #1
Quiz - Distribute quizzes and give students about 10 minutes to complete them. (NOTE: The quizzes may either be the short answer study guides or the multiple choice version for chapters 7-8.) Have students exchange papers. Grade the quizzes as a class. Collect the papers for recording the grades. (If you used the multiple choice version as a quiz, take a few minutes to discuss the answers for the short answer version if your students are using the short answer version for their study guides.)

Activity #2
Tell students to preview the study questions and do the vocabulary work for chapters 9-10. Give students about 15 minutes for this activity.

Activity #3
Tell students that they should read chapters 9-10 prior to your next class meeting. If they have time after completing Activity #2, they may use the remainder of this class period to begin their reading.

LESSON SEVEN

Objectives
1. To check to see that students did the required reading assignment
2. To review the main ideas of chapters 9-10
3. To preview the study questions for chapters 11-12
4. To read chapters 11-12

Activity #1

Quiz - Distribute quizzes and give students about 10 minutes to complete them. (NOTE: The quizzes may either be the short answer study guides or the multiple choice version for chapters 9-10.) Have students exchange papers. Grade the quizzes as a class. Collect the papers for recording the grades. (If you used the multiple choice version as a quiz, take a few minutes to discuss the answers for the short answer version if your students are using the short answer version for their study guides.)

Activity #2

Tell students to preview the study questions and do the vocabulary work for chapters 11-12. Give students about 15 minutes for this activity.

Activity #3

Tell students that they should read chapters 11-12 prior to your next class meeting. If they have time after completing Activity #2, they may use the remainder of this class period to begin their reading.

LESSON EIGHT

Objectives
1. To review the main ideas and events from chapters 11-12
2. To discuss *Roll of Thunder, Hear My Cry* on interpretive and critical levels

Activity #1

Take a few minutes at the beginning of the period to review the study questions for chapters 11-12.

Activity #2

Choose the questions from the Extra Discussion Questions/Writing Assignments which seem most appropriate for your students. A class discussion of these questions is most effective if students have been given the opportunity to formulate answers to the questions prior to the discussion. To this end, you may either have all the students formulate answers to all the questions, divide your class into groups and assign one or more questions to each group, or assign one question to each student in your class. The option you choose will make a difference in the amount of class time needed for this activity.

Activity #3

After students have had ample time to formulate answers to the questions, begin your class discussion of the questions and the ideas presented by the questions. Be sure students take notes during the discussion so they have information to study for the unit test.

EXTRA WRITING ASSIGNMENTS/DISCUSSION QUESTIONS
Roll of Thunder, Hear My Cry

<u>Interpretation</u>

1. Explain how Mildred D. Taylor's using Cassie as the narrator affects our understanding of the events in *Roll of Thunder, Hear My Cry*.

2. What are the main conflicts in the story, and how are they resolved?

3. What is the setting of the story? How is it important to the themes in the novel?

4. Where is the climax of the story? Justify your answer.

5. Cite as many examples of Mary Logan's strength of character as you can find.

<u>Critical</u>

6. Explain Mildred D. Taylor's use of thunder, rain, forest/woods, darkness and light in *Roll of Thunder, Hear My Cry*.

7. Are the characters' actions believably motivated? Explain why or why not.

8. Compare and contrast Uncle Hammer and David Logan.

9. Evaluate Mildred D. Taylor's style of writing. How does it contribute to the value of the novel?

10. Why did the author bring in Mr. Morrison? What was his use as a character?

11. Classify these people as "good guys" or "bad guys": Mr. Granger, Silas Avery, Kaleb Wallace, Mr. Grimes, Mr. Jamison, Mr. Barnett, Mr. Simms, R.W. and Melvin. Explain your classifications.

12. Why was the land so important?

13. Explain how the title relates to the events of the novel and the themes of *Roll of Thunder, Hear My Cry*.

14. Miss Crocker "had looked at the page and had understood nothing." What should she have understood?

15. T.J. said, "Friends gotta trust each other, Stacey, 'cause ain't nothin' like a true friend." Did T.J. live by his own words? If so, how? If not, why not?

Roll of Thunder, Hear My Cry Extra Discussion Questions page 2

16. Are the characters in *Roll of Thunder, Hear My Cry* stereotypes? If so, explain why Mildred D. Taylor used stereotypes. If not, explain how the characters merit individuality.

17. Why did David Logan set fire to the cotton?

18. What was Jeremy's use as a character?

19. Compare and contrast the children with their parents in these families: Logan, Avery and Simms.

Critical/Personal Response

20. Who is responsible for T.J.'s downfall? Justify your answer.

21. Why did Mr. Morrison let Stacey decide whether or not to tell Mama about fighting at the Wallaces' store? Why did Stacey decide to tell her?

22. What faults in our society does Mildred D. Taylor point out in *Roll of Thunder*?

23. Do you think the sibling relationships among the Logan children are realistic? Explain why or why not.

24. Cassie said (about Mr. Barnett), "You know he was wrong!" Stacey replied, "I know it and you know it, but he don't know it, and that's where the trouble is." About whom in the story (besides Mr. Barnett) could this conversation have been? Give all possible responses and justify your answers.

25. Why didn't Lillian Jean understand why Cassie punched her?

Personal Response

26. Did you enjoy reading *Roll of Thunder, Hear My Cry*? Why or why not?

27. What is freedom?

28. Suppose the story had been written from Little Man's point of view. How would that have changed our perception of the events?

29. Do things like those that happened to Cassie and her family in the story still happen today?

30. Do you think people's prejudices can or will ever be overcome? Explain why or why not.

LESSON NINE

Objective
To review all of the vocabulary work done in this unit

Activity
Choose one (or more) of the vocabulary review activities listed below and spend your class period as directed in the activity. Some of the materials for these review activities are located in the Vocabulary Resource section of this unit.

VOCABULARY REVIEW ACTIVITIES

1. Divide your class into two teams and have an old-fashioned spelling or definition bee.

2. Give each of your students (or students in groups of two, three or four) a *Roll of Thunder, Hear My Cry* Vocabulary Word Search Puzzle. The person (group) to find all of the vocabulary words in the puzzle first wins.

3. Give students a *Roll of Thunder, Hear My Cry* Vocabulary Word Search Puzzle without the word list. The person or group to find the most vocabulary words in the puzzle wins.

4. Use a *Roll of Thunder, Hear My Cry* Vocabulary Crossword Puzzle. Put the puzzle onto a transparency on the overhead projector (so everyone can see it), and do the puzzle together as a class.

5. Give students a *Roll of Thunder, Hear My Cry* Vocabulary Matching Worksheet to do.

6. Divide your class into two teams. Use the *Roll of Thunder, Hear My Cry* vocabulary words with their letters jumbled as a word list. Student 1 from Team A faces off against Student 1 from Team B. You write the first jumbled word on the board. The first student (1A or 1B) to unscramble the word wins the chance for his/her team to score points. If 1A wins the jumble, go to student 2A and give him/her a definition. He/she must give you the correct spelling of the vocabulary word which fits that definition. If he/she does, Team A scores a point, and you give student 3A a definition for which you expect a correctly spelled matching vocabulary word. Continue giving Team A definitions until some team member makes an incorrect response. An incorrect response sends the game back to the jumbled-word face off, this time with students 2A and 2B. Instead of repeating giving definitions to the first few students of each team, continue with the student after the one who gave the last incorrect response on the team. For example, if Team B wins the jumbled-word face-off, and student 5B gave the last incorrect answer for Team B, you would start this round of definition questions with student 6B, and so on. The team with the most points wins!

7. Have students write a story in which they correctly use as many vocabulary words as possible. Have students read their compositions orally! Post the most original compositions on your bulletin board.

LESSON TEN

Objectives

1. To check students' understanding of the motives of the characters
2. To give students the opportunity to practice writing to persuade
3. To give the teacher the opportunity to evaluate students' writing

Activity

Distribute Writing Assignment #2. Discuss the directions in detail and give students ample time to complete the assignment.

Follow up with a writing conference after you have read the students' papers. This unit schedules writing conference time in Lesson Thirteen.

WRITING ASSIGNMENT #2 - *Roll of Thunder, Hear My Cry*

PROMPT
The boycott of the Wallaces' store is an important part of the book. Its success depends on Mrs. Logan's ability to convince people that the boycott will be worthwhile even though it will cause significant hardships for those who participate.

Your assignment is to write a composition in which you pretend you are Mrs. Logan and are attempting to persuade one of your neighbors to boycott the Wallaces' store.

PREWRITING
The first thing you need to do is to make a list of all the reasons why members of the community should boycott the store: What brought about the need for a boycott? What is the purpose of the boycott? What effect will the boycott have on Mr. Wallace? What good will come of the boycott?

Next, think about how the boycott will affect your neighbor. Jot down all the possible negative effects of the boycott on your neighbor. These will be the objections you will have to overcome with your arguments.

DRAFTING
Start with a paragraph in which you introduce the topic of the boycott of Mr. Wallace's store. This might be a good place to include the information about what brought about the need for a boycott.

There are several ways to organize your ideas. One way is to take the objections your neighbor will have and overcome each objection with positive facts about the benefits of the boycott. So your paper would go: introduction, objection/benefit, objection/benefit, objection/benefit, etc., conclusion.

Another way to organize your ideas would be to put forth your arguments, then recognize the objections and overcome them by briefly restating the appropriate benefits or by finding other ways to trivialize the objections so that they seem less significant compared to the benefits of the boycott. So your paper would go: introduction, benefit, benefit, benefit, recognize an objection/overcome the objection, recognize an objection/overcome the objection, etc., conclusion.

Yet another way to organize your ideas would be to introduce the idea of a boycott, recognize all of the objections, and then state all of the benefits. So your paper would go: introduction, paragraph of objections, benefits, benefits, benefits, benefits, etc., conclusion.

Choose whichever of these methods that seems to best fit your material and your writing style.

PROMPT
When you finish the rough draft of your paper, ask a student who sits near you to read it. After reading your rough draft, he/she should tell you what he/she liked best about your work, which parts were difficult to understand, and ways in which your work could be improved. Reread your paper considering your critic's comments and make the corrections you think are necessary.

PROOFREADING
Do a final proofreading of your paper double-checking your grammar, spelling, organization, and the clarity of your ideas.

LESSONS ELEVEN AND TWELVE

Objectives
    1. To discuss major themes and ideas of *Roll of Thunder, Hear My Cry*
    2. To give students the opportunity to practice working together in small groups

Activity #1
    Divide your class into groups - one group for each of the following topics:
    1. INJUSTICE: What events in the book were "not fair," as Cassie would say? What injustices were done in the book, and how did they affect the people involved?

    2. NAIVETE; "GROWING UP": What things happened in the book to take away children's innocence or to make someone "grow up" a little bit? What harsh realities did the characters have to face?

    3. REVENGE: There are many references to getting even or getting revenge in the story. What were they? Were they successful? What effect did they have on the people involved?

    4. FRIENDSHIP: There are many different kinds of "friendships" in the story. Choose pairs of characters and describe their relationships. A few examples would be Cassie/Lillian Jean, Jeremy/Logan kids, T.J./Stacey, and Mr. Morrison/the Logans. There are many others you should explore as well.

    5. PRIDE/DIGNITY: There are many events in the story which involve pride or dignity. What are they? What do they show?

    6. DUTY: Many actions in the story are done out of duty or responsibility rather than from desire. What are they? Who did them? Why?

NOTE: If students will divide the chapters of the book up among themselves, assigning one or two chapters to each student, the researching portion of the work will go faster. They should then get together and put together all of the information they have found and discuss it.

Activity #2
    Allow the groups time to research and discuss their topics. Each group should appoint a spokesperson to report the group's thoughts.

Activity #3
    Ask each group's spokesperson to give the group's thoughts about the topic. Jot these down on the board or overhead projector and use them as a springboard for a discussion of the topics.

LESSON THIRTEEN

Objectives
1. To give students the opportunity to explore nonfiction topics related to the story
2. To give students the opportunity to use the library
3. To broaden students' knowledge of our world

Activity

Take students to the library. Explain to them that this is their opportunity to complete the nonfiction reading assignment which accompanies this unit. Students are to find nonfiction books or articles in some way relating to *Roll of Thunder, Hear My Cry*. Students are to use this time to find nonfiction materials that interest them and to begin reading. Remind students to complete the Nonfiction Assignment Sheet after they have done their reading.

Remind students that they will be giving a little oral report about their nonfiction reading in the next class period.

Suggested Topics:
- Biography of Mildred D. Taylor
- Articles about *Roll of Thunder, Hear My Cry*
- Land value
- Mortgages
- Civil Rights
- Cotton farming
- U.S. history 1930-1940
- Ways to improve one's life
- Careers in farming, retail business, banking, education
- Boycotts
- Agencies that help people fight injustice
- Articles about overcoming prejudice
- Current problems facing black Americans
- Desegregation of schools
- Education
- Taking pride in yourself and your work

LESSON FOURTEEN

<u>Objectives</u>
1. To broaden students' knowledge of our world
2. To give students a little information about many topics related to the story
3. To give students the opportunity to practice public speaking
4. To evaluate students' retention of the nonfiction they read

<u>Activity</u>

Have each student stand in front of the class to give a short summary of the nonfiction he/she read relating to *Roll of Thunder, Hear My Cry*.

NOTE: The point is not to embarrass anyone; rather, to encourage students to be able to think on their feet, to be able to express themselves verbally even when they are in front of a group of people. This is a valuable skill for students to develop to help them prepare for adult life. As adults, they will need to be able to stand up and express their opinions or give out a little information whether they are at a PTA meeting, a meeting at work, or in one of hundreds of other possible scenarios.

In addition, by hearing all the other reports, students will be exposed to all kinds of information instead of just their own reading.

LESSON FIFTEEN

Objectives
1. To broaden students' understanding of our world
2. To show students what is involved in buying real estate in real life today
3. To relate a main idea from the novel to a real-life situation

Activity

Invite one of your local real estate brokers to come to your classroom to explain to students what is involved when one wants to purchase residential real estate. If possible, the broker should bring a large selection of properties for sale complete with descriptions and photos. (They do not have to be homes currently on the market; some old multiple listing books would do.) Distribute the information about properties for sale at the beginning of the period and let students choose the property they would like to "purchase" during this class period.

Have the broker describe the steps one must take to purchase the property. Let students "walk through" the process using the properties they have decided to "buy."

Students should be able to figure out how much money they will need for a down payment, how much they will need for settlement costs, and how much they will need each year for taxes.

You can make this project as elaborate as you wish. You could create a whole host of writing assignments and activities related to this project. Some ideas: calculating how much money it will take to run the household, descriptive essay describing the house to relatives or friends who live far away, letters of complaint regarding undisclosed repairs that need to be made after the student "moves in," a discussion of homeowners' insurance, a shopping spree to furnish and decorate the house, costs of moving and how to move, miscellaneous items about moving into a new house such as how to get a telephone or cable TV connected, fuel oil/propane delivery, garbage disposal (finding a trash collector if you don't live in the city), changing your address for bills, magazines, checking accounts, credit cards, and driver's license, etc.

LESSON SIXTEEN

<u>Objectives</u>
1. To relate an idea from the novel to a real-life situation
2. To broaden students' understanding of our world

<u>Activity #1</u>
Divide your class into four groups. Assign each group three chapters of the novel. With each group, students should search their three chapters for items one could purchase. For example, Hammer's car, 400 acres of land, a new coat, a new suit, groceries, books, repairs to a bus stuck in the mud with a broken axle, shoes, etc.

<u>Activity #2</u>
After students have found items in the text, have each group report its findings. Make a composite list of items on the board or overhead projector and have students copy down the list on paper.

<u>Activity #3</u>
Have students return to their groups. Their task this time will be to estimate the cost of each of the items on the list. Through their discussions, students should try to come up with the most accurate number possible.

<u>Activity #4</u>
Have the groups report their results and write the results on the board next to the items you have listed.

<u>Activity #5</u>
Assign each student one item on the list. Prior to your next class meeting students should find the actual price for their items. Perhaps you could make a prize of some sort for the group who came the closest in their total cost estimation.

LESSONS SEVENTEEN AND EIGHTEEN

Objectives
1. To give students the opportunity to express their personal opinions
2. To help students become more responsible for themselves
3. To relate an idea in the book to a real-life situation

Activity #1

Have students report the actual prices of the items they were to find. Tally up the actual prices and the estimates for each group and award a prize to the group members who had the closest estimate.

Activity #2

Distribute Writing Assignment #3. Discuss the directions in detail and give students ample time to complete the assignment.

LESSON NINETEEN

Objective
To review the main ideas presented in *Roll of Thunder, Hear My Cry*

Activity #1

Choose one of the review games/activities included in this unit and spend your class period as outlined there. Some materials for these activities are located in the Extra Activities section of this unit.

Activity #2

Remind students that the Unit Test will be in the next class meeting. Stress the review of the Study Guides and their class notes as a last minute, brush-up review for homework.

WRITING ASSIGNMENT #3 - *Roll of Thunder, Hear My Cry*

PROMPT

"Baby, we have no choice of what color we're born or who our parents are or whether we're rich or poor. What we do have is some choice over what we make of our lives once we're here."

Mama's words to Cassie are appropriate for all of us. We all have to take responsibility for our own lives, to make the best of the cards we're dealt, so to speak. We all have strengths and weaknesses, talents and shortcomings, things in our favor and things against us. It is our job to do the best we can with our own situations.

Your assignment is to write a composition in which you express your own aspirations and make a reasonable plan as to how to realize them.

PREWRITING

Jot down some notes to help you get started. First, try answering these questions: What do you want to do with the rest of your life? What good things do you have going for you? What kinds of things are against you or not in your favor? How can you overcome or circumvent the obstacles between you and your goals? What do you need to do to realize your goals?

Take your time with the prewriting stage. Don't just write down any old thing; put some thought and effort into figuring out what you want to do and how you can do it.

DRAFTING

One way to write this paper is to begin with an introductory statement in which you introduce the idea of what you do want to do with the rest of your life. In the body of your plan, write a section about the things you have in your favor, then a section about the things you will have to overcome, and then a section telling how you can overcome the problems. Write a section in which you spell out your plan of action. Finally, write your concluding statement to end your plan. This is just a general guideline as to one way to write your paper. Label each section clearly: <u>Introduction</u>, <u>Things In My Favor</u>, <u>Things To Overcome</u>, <u>Ways To Overcome Obstacles</u>, <u>My Plan</u>, and <u>Conclusion</u>.

PROMPT

When you finish the rough draft of your paper, ask a student who sits near you to read it. After reading your rough draft, he/she should tell you what he/she liked best about your work, which parts were difficult to understand, and ways in which your work could be improved. Reread your paper considering your critic's comments and make the corrections you think are necessary.

PROOFREADING

Do a final proofreading of your paper double-checking your grammar, spelling, organization, and the clarity of your ideas.

REVIEW GAMES/ACTIVITIES - *Roll of Thunder, Hear My Cry*

1. Ask the class to make up a unit test for *Roll of Thunder, Hear My Cry*. The test should have 4 sections: matching, true/false, short answer, and essay. Students may use 1/2 period to make the test and then swap papers and use the other 1/2 class period to take a test a classmate has devised. (open book). You may want to use the unit test included in this unit or take questions from the students' unit tests to formulate your own test.

2. Take 1/2 period for students to make up true and false questions (including the answers). Collect the papers and divide the class into two teams. Draw a big tic-tac-toe board on the chalk board. Make one team X and one team O. Ask questions to each side, giving each student one turn. If the question is answered correctly, that students' team's letter (X or O) is placed in the box. If the answer is incorrect, no mark is placed in the box. The object is to get three marks in a row like tic-tac-toe. You may want to keep track of the number of games won for each team.

3. Take 1/2 period for students to make up questions (true/false and short answer). Collect the questions. Divide the class into two teams. You'll alternate asking questions to individual members of teams A & B (like in a spelling bee). The question keeps going from A to B until it is correctly answered, then a new question is asked. A correct answer does not allow the team to get another question. Correct answers are +2 points; incorrect answers are -1 point.

4. Have students pair up and quiz each other from their study guides and class notes.

5. Give students a *Roll of Thunder, Hear My Cry* crossword puzzle to complete.

6. Divide your class into two teams. Use the *Roll of Thunder, Hear My Cry* crossword words with their letters jumbled as a word list. Student 1 from Team A faces off against Student 1 from Team B. You write the first jumbled word on the board. The first student (1A or 1B) to unscramble the word wins the chance for his/her team to score points. If 1A wins the jumble, go to student 2A and give him/her a clue. He/she must give you the correct word which matches that clue. If he/she does, Team A scores a point, and you give student 3A a clue for which you expect another correct response. Continue giving Team A clues until some team member makes an incorrect response. An incorrect response sends the game back to the jumbled-word face off, this time with students 2A and 2B. Instead of repeating giving clues to the first few students of each team, continue with the student after the one who gave the last incorrect response on the team. For example, if Team B wins the jumbled-word face-off, and student 5B gave the last incorrect answer for Team B, you would start this round of clue questions with student 6B, and so on. The team with the most points wins!

UNIT TESTS

SHORT ANSWER UNIT TEST 1 - *Roll of Thunder, Hear My Cry*

I. Matching/Identify

___ 1. Jeremy   A. Big Ma's husband; he bought the land

___ 2. Little Man   B. R.W. & Melvin beat him up

___ 3. Cassie   C. Clayton Chester; he liked to be clean

___ 4. Hammer   D. Big, strong friend of the Logan family

___ 5. Paul Edward   E. The horse

___ 6. Taylor   F. Cassie punched her

___ 7. T.J.   G. He drove a Packard like Mr. Granger's

___ 8. Jack   H. Lawyer friend of the Logans

___ 9. Caroline   I. White boy friendly towards the Logans

___ 10. Wallace   J. Store owner

___ 11. Morrison   K. Big Ma

___ 12. Lillian Jean   L. Rich land owner

___ 13. Stacey   M. Narrator

___ 14. Jamison   N. Felt responsible for Papa's broken leg

___ 15. Granger   O. Author

Roll of Thunder Short Answer Unit Test 1 Page 2

II. Short Answer
1. Why did Cassie and Little Man refuse to take their readers?

2. Why didn't Papa want the children to go to the Wallaces' store?

3. Why did the Logan children dig a hole in the road?

4. Who were the "riders," and what were they doing?

5. Why had Papa hired Mr. Morrison?

6. Why did Mama try to convince Mr. Turner to stop shopping at the Wallaces' store?

7. What made Cassie yell at Mr. Barnett?

8. Why did Cassie take Lillian Jean into the woods?

Roll of Thunder Short Answer Unit Test 1 Page 3

9. Why did Mama lose her teaching job?

10. Why did the Logans finally have to depend on Uncle Hammer for money?

11. What happened to T.J.?

12. What stopped the mob from lynching T.J.?

III. Composition
   Why did Cassie cry "For T.J. and the land"?

Roll of Thunder Short Answer Unit Test 1 Page 4

IV. Vocabulary
	Listen to the vocabulary words and write them down.
	Go back later and write in definitions for the words.

1.

2.

3.

4.

5.

6.

7.

8.

9.

10.

SHORT ANSWER UNIT TEST 2 - *Roll of Thunder, Hear My Cry*

I. Matching

___ 1. Jeremy   A. Clayton Chester; he liked to be clean

___ 2. Little Man   B. Big, strong friend of the Logan family

___ 3. Cassie   C. Big Ma's husband; he bought the land

___ 4. Hammer   D. R.W. & Melvin beat him up

___ 5. Paul Edward   E. He drove a Packard like Mr. Granger's

___ 6. Taylor   F. Lawyer friend of the Logans

___ 7. T.J.   G. The horse

___ 8. Jack   H. Cassie punched her

___ 9. Caroline   I. Big Ma

___ 10. Wallace   J. Rich land owner

___ 11. Morrison   K. Narrator

___ 12. Lillian Jean   L. Store owner

___ 13. Stacey   M. White boy friendly towards the Logans

___ 14. Jamison   N. Author

___ 15. Granger   O. Felt responsible for Papa's broken leg

Roll of Thunder Short Answer Unit Test 2 Page 2

II. Short Answer

1. How did Mary Logan react to Daisy's news about the children's refusal to accept the books?

2. What was the problem with the Jefferson Davis school bus?

3. What did Mama do when she found out that the children had been at the Wallaces' store?

4. Why was Cassie mad at Big Ma after the trip to Strawberry?

5. What papers did Big Ma sign?

6. Why did Mr. Jamison want to back the people's credit?

7. Why did Cassie take Lillian Jean into the woods?

8. Why didn't Papa want to borrow money from Hammer?

9. What stopped the mob?

Roll of Thunder Short Answer Unit Test 2 Page 3

III. Composition

Big Ma, Mary Logan, David Logan, Uncle Hammer, and Mr. Morrison all provided valuable examples and/or advice for young Cassie. Tell what lesson each of these characters provided for Cassie. Explain each thoroughly.

Roll of Thunder Short Answer Unit Test 2 Page 4

IV. Vocabulary
    Listen to the vocabulary words and write them down.
    Go back later and write in definitions for the words.

1.

2.

3.

4.

5.

6.

7.

8.

9.

10.

KEY: SHORT ANSWER UNIT TESTS - *Roll of Thunder, Hear My Cry*

The short answer questions are taken directly from the study guides.
If you need to look up the answers, you will find them in the study guide section.

Answers to the composition questions will vary depending on your
class discussions and the level of your students.

For the vocabulary section of the test, choose ten of the
words from the vocabulary lists to read orally for your students.

The answers to the matching section of the test are below.

Answers to the matching section of the Advanced Short Answer Unit Test
are the same as for Short Answer Unit Test #2.

Test #1	Test #2
1. I	1. M
2. C	2. A
3. M	3. K
4. G	4. E
5. A	5. C
6. O	6. N
7. B	7. D
8. E	8. G
9. K	9. I
10. J	10. L
11. D	11. B
12. F	12. H
13. N	13. O
14. H	14. F
15. L	15. J

ADVANCED SHORT ANSWER UNIT TEST - *Roll of Thunder, Hear My Cry*

I. Matching/Identify

___ 1. Jeremy   A. Clayton Chester; he liked to be clean

___ 2. Little Man   B. Big, strong friend of the Logan family

___ 3. Cassie   C. Big Ma's husband; he bought the land

___ 4. Hammer   D. R.W. & Melvin beat him up

___ 5. Paul Edward   E. He drove a Packard like Mr. Granger's

___ 6. Taylor   F. Lawyer friend of the Logans

___ 7. T.J.   G. The horse

___ 8. Jack   H. Cassie punched her

___ 9. Caroline   I. Big Ma

___ 10. Wallace   J. Rich land owner

___ 11. Morrison   K. Narrator

___ 12. Lillian Jean   L. Store owner

___ 13. Stacey   M. White boy friendly towards the Logans

___ 14. Jamison   N. Author

___ 15. Granger   O. Felt responsible for Papa's broken leg

Roll of Thunder Advanced Short Answer Unit Test Page 2

II. Short Answer

1. Cite at least three examples of Mary Logan's strength of character.

2. Compare and contrast Uncle Hammer and David Logan.

3. Why was the land so important?

4. Miss Crocker "had looked at the page and had understood nothing." What should she have understood?

5. T.J. said, "Friends gotta trust each other, Stacey, 'cause ain't nothin' like a true friend." Did T.J. live by his own words? If so, how? If not, why not?

6. Why did David Logan set fire to the cotton?

Roll of Thunder Advanced Short Answer Unit Test Page 3

7. What was Jeremy's use as a character?

8. Who is responsible for T.J.'s downfall? Justify your answer.

9. Why didn't Lillian Jean understand why Cassie punched her?

III. Essay
    What faults in our society did Mildred D. Taylor point out in *Roll of Thunder*? Explain in detail how each was brought out in the story.

Roll of Thunder Advanced Short Answer Unit Test Page 4

IV. Vocabulary

    Listen to the words and write them down. Go back later and write a composition using all of the vocabulary words you were given. The composition must relate in some way to *Roll of Thunder*.

MULTIPLE CHOICE UNIT TEST 1 - *Roll of Thunder, Hear My Cry*

I. Matching

___ 1. Jeremy   A. Big Ma's husband; he bought the land

___ 2. Little Man   B. R.W. & Melvin beat him up

___ 3. Cassie   C. Clayton Chester; he liked to be clean

___ 4. Hammer   D. Big, strong friend of the Logan family

___ 5. Paul Edward   E. The horse

___ 6. Taylor   F. Cassie punched her

___ 7. T.J.   G. He drove a Packard like Mr. Granger's

___ 8. Jack   H. Lawyer friend of the Logans

___ 9. Caroline   I. White boy friendly towards the Logans

___ 10. Wallace   J. Store owner

___ 11. Morrison   K. Big Ma

___ 12. Lillian Jean   L. Rich land owner

___ 13. Stacey   M. Narrator

___ 14. Jamison   N. Felt responsible for Papa's broken leg

___ 15. Granger   O. Author

Roll of Thunder Multiple Choice Unit Test 1 Page 2

II. Multiple Choice

1. Which of these statements describes Cassie?
    A. She is a fourth grade student who despises dressing up and sticks up for her own rights.
    B. She is a seventh grade student who is very belligerent and is in constant conflict with her parents and teachers.
    C. She is a fifth grade student who is very shy and rarely speaks to anyone.
    D. She is a first grade student who is bright and learned to read at an early age.

2. Why did Cassie and Little Man refuse to take their readers?
    A. In the front of the books, the black students were called "nigra." The books were handed down from the white school and were in poor condition.
    B. They had both seen dead bugs inside the readers and were afraid of finding more.
    C. They were embarrassed to admit that they could not read.
    D. They were afraid Big Ma would whip them for reading anything but the Bible.

3. Why didn't Papa want the children to go to the Wallaces' store?
    A. People went there to drink and carouse, and the children usually ended up in trouble. It wasn't a wholesome place for children.
    B. Papa thought that music and dancing were sinful. He did not want his children to associate with sinners.
    C. The store was a long way from home. He didn't want them to walk that far.
    D. He was afraid the children would act up and embarrass him.

4. What was the problem with the Jefferson Davis school bus?
    A. It was old and broke down at least once a week, and the white students didn't want to walk to school with the black students.
    B. The new driver was black. Some of the white students refused to ride without a white driver..
    C. The driver would run the black children off the road so the white children could jeer at them.
    D. It was supposed to pick up the black students, but the driver didn't always stop.

5. Why did the Logan children dig a hole in the road?
    A. They thought it would help drain the water away from the bank.
    B. They wanted to get even with the bus driver and kids by causing the bus to get stuck.
    C. They thought the road would flood and then they would not have to go to school for a few days.
    D. T.J. had offered them money to do it. He wanted Mr. Granger's car to get muddy.

Roll of Thunder Multiple Choice Unit Test 1 Page 3

6. Who were the "riders," and what were they doing?
    A. They were the white students who were brought to school by horse and wagon while the bus was being repaired.
    B. They were a gang of white men who rode in a convoy of cars out to the black neighborhoods to burn and hurt the black people who had supposedly stepped out of their place.
    C. They were a group of black men who rode through the area on horseback delivering mail and supplies to people in the area.
    D. They were the railroad bosses who rode over the newly laid track to inspect it. If they didn't like it, the workers didn't get paid.

7. What did Mama do when she found out that the children had been at the Wallaces' store?
    A. She whipped them and sent them to their rooms.
    B. She took them to see Mr. Berry, who had been burned by the Wallaces.
    C. She cried and told them how hard it was for her when her husband was gone.
    D. She said she would not help them if they got into trouble at the store.

8. Why did Mama try to convince Mr. Turner to stop shopping at the Wallaces' store?
    A. She wanted him to shop around for lower prices.
    B. She thought he was spending too much money and should save some.
    C. She was trying to organize a boycott of the store to protest the burnings.
    D. She wanted him to give money to the church instead.

9. Why was Cassie disappointed in Strawberry?
    A. She had expected Strawberry to be a bigger, more modern city than it was.
    B. She thought there would be plenty of strawberry dishes to eat, and that was her favorite fruit.
    C. It was crowded and noisy. She liked wide open spaces.
    D. Big Ma didn't let her do anything but sit in the wagon.

10. What made Cassie yell at Mr. Barnett?
    A. She could see that a sack of flour was going to fall off the shelf onto his head, and she wanted him to get out of the way.
    B. She was angry that he waited on a white child who had come in the store after them.
    C. He said he would only sell candy to white children.
    D. She didn't think he should have guns on display in the front counter.

Roll of Thunder Multiple Choice Unit Test 1 Page 4

11. Why was Cassie mad at Big Ma?
    A. Big Ma refused to buy her candy or pretty hair ribbons.
    B. She wanted to drive the wagon home, but Big Ma said no.
    C. Big Ma made her apologize to Lillian Jean.
    D. Big Ma would not let her visit with Mr. Jamison and his family.

12. Why didn't Papa want to back people's credit with his land?
    A. He didn't really like his neighbors enough to do that for them.
    B. If the people couldn't pay their bills, he would have to sell his land for the bills he guaranteed.
    C. Mama said she would not speak to him if he did it.
    D. He was afraid of what the white men might do to him.

13. What papers did Big Ma sign?
    A. An agreement to back the neighbors' credit
    B. A formal complaint against Mr. Simms for hurting Cassie
    C. A title transfer to give the land to Papa and Uncle Hammer
    D. A contract donating part of her forest to the church

14. Why did Cassie take Lillian Jean into the woods?
    A. There were some beautiful wildflowers that Cassie knew Lillian Jean would like to see.
    B. Cassie planned to get Lillian Jean lost and then leave her there to scare her.
    C. Cassie didn't want any witnesses to see that she and Lillian Jean were fighting.
    D. Cassie had built a secret tree house that she wanted to show to Lillian Jean.

15. Why did Mama lose her teaching job?
    A. There weren't enough students in the seventh grade, so the principal had to fire one teacher and put the students in another class.
    B. The school board didn't think she should be teaching in the same school that her children attended.
    C. She was not supposed to whip the students, but she did it anyway.
    D. She was not teaching what was in the history books, and she was stirring up trouble with the boycott.

16. What stopped the mob?
    A. Mr. Jamison finally convinced them he was right.
    B. They all went to fight the fire in the cotton field.
    C. The sheriff and his deputies threatened to arrest them all.
    D. The Simms boys told the truth.

Roll of Thunder Multiple Choice Unit Test 1 Page 5

III. Composition

> *Roll of Thunder, Hear My Cry* has been called "a story of the survival of the human spirit." Explain why/how this statement is true.

Roll of Thunder Multiple Choice Unit Test 1 Page 6

IV. Vocabulary Match the words with the correct definitions.

___ 1. MINGLING   A. mixing together

___ 2. CONCESSION   B. impossible to reach or enter

___ 3. UNDAUNTED   C. unaware of; not mindful of

___ 4. OBLIVIOUS   D. boiling over with anger

___ 5. APPREHENSIVE   E. returned like for like

___ 6. RETALIATED   F. portentous; foreboding

___ 7. FEIGNED   G. ignored; kept out of association with

___ 8. LOITERING   H. able or quick to understand

___ 9. OMINOUSLY   I. at a distance; removed

___ 10. SHROUD   J. hanging around with nothing particular to do

___ 11. CONDESCENDING   K. a gradual increase in loudness or intensity

___ 12. SHUNNED   L. something that conceals or screens like a garment

___ 13. INACCESSIBLE   M. pretended

___ 14. OBVIOUS   N. not faltering or hesitating

___ 15. FUMING   O. a compromise

___ 16. MUTELY   P. without speaking

___ 17. PLACID   Q. tranquil; calm

___ 18. CONDONED   R. easy to see or understand

___ 19. CRESCENDO   S. endorsed; gave approval for

___ 20. ALOOFNESS   T. descending voluntarily to the level of an inferior person

MULTIPLE CHOICE UNIT TEST 2 - *Roll of Thunder, Hear My Cry*

I. Matching

___ 1. Jeremy   A. Clayton Chester; he liked to be clean

___ 2. Little Man   B. Big, strong friend of the Logan family

___ 3. Cassie   C. Big Ma's husband; he bought the land

___ 4. Hammer   D. R.W. & Melvin beat him up

___ 5. Paul Edward   E. He drove a Packard like Mr. Granger's

___ 6. Taylor   F. Lawyer friend of the Logans

___ 7. T.J.   G. The horse

___ 8. Jack   H. Cassie punched her

___ 9. Caroline   I. Big Ma

___ 10. Wallace   J. Rich land owner

___ 11. Morrison   K. Narrator

___ 12. Lillian Jean   L. Store owner

___ 13. Stacey   M. White boy friendly towards the Logans

___ 14. Jamison   N. Author

___ 15. Granger   O. Felt responsible for Papa's broken leg

Roll of Thunder Multiple Choice Unit Test 2 Page 2

II. Multiple Choice

1. Which of these statements describes Cassie?
    - A. She is a fifth grade student who is very shy and rarely speaks to anyone.
    - B. She is a seventh grade student who is very belligerent and is in constant conflict with her parents and teachers.
    - C. She is a fourth grade student who despises dressing up and sticks up for her own rights.
    - D. She is a first grade student who is bright and learned to read at an early age.

2. Why did Cassie and Little Man refuse to take their readers?
    - A. They had both seen dead bugs inside the readers and were afraid of finding more.
    - B. In the front of the books, the black students were called "nigra." The books were handed down from the white school and were in poor condition.
    - C. They were embarrassed to admit that they could not read.
    - D. They were afraid Big Ma would whip them for reading anything but the Bible.

3. Why didn't Papa want the children to go to the Wallaces' store?
    - A. He was afraid the children would act up and embarrass him.
    - B. Papa thought that music and dancing were sinful. He did not want his children to associate with sinners.
    - C. The store was a long way from home. He didn't want them to walk that far.
    - D. People went there to drink and carouse, and the children usually ended up in trouble. It wasn't a wholesome place for children.

4. What was the problem with the Jefferson Davis school bus?
    - A. The driver would run the black children off the road so the white children could jeer at them.
    - B. The new driver was black. Some of the white students refused to ride without a white driver..
    - C. It was old and broke down at least once a week, and the white students didn't want to walk to school with the black students.
    - D. It was supposed to pick up the black students, but the driver didn't always stop.

5. Why did the Logan children dig a hole in the road?
    - A. They thought it would help drain the water away from the bank.
    - B. T.J. had offered them money to do it. He wanted Mr. Granger's car to get muddy.
    - C. They thought the road would flood and then they would not have to go to school for a few days.
    - D. They wanted to get even with the bus driver and kids by causing the bus to get stuck.

Roll of Thunder Multiple Choice Unit Test 2 Page 3

6. Who were the "riders," and what were they doing?
    A. They were the white students who were brought to school by horse and wagon while the bus was being repaired.
    B. They were a group of black men who rode through the area on horseback delivering mail and supplies to people in the area.
    C. They were a gang of white men who rode in a convoy of cars out to the black neighborhoods to burn and hurt the black people who had supposedly stepped out of their place.
    D. They were the railroad bosses who rode over the newly laid track to inspect it. If they didn't like it, the workers didn't get paid.

7. What did Mama do when she found out that the children had been at the Wallaces' store?
    A. She took them to see Mr. Berry, who had been burned by the Wallaces.
    B. She whipped them and sent them to their rooms.
    C. She cried and told them how hard it was for her when her husband was gone.
    D. She said she would not help them if they got into trouble at the store.

8. Why did Mama try to convince Mr. Turner to stop shopping at the Wallaces' store?
    A. She wanted him to shop around for lower prices.
    B. She was trying to organize a boycott of the store to protest the burnings.
    C. She thought he was spending too much money and should save some.
    D. She wanted him to give money to the church instead.

9. Why was Cassie disappointed in Strawberry?
    A. It was crowded and noisy. She liked wide open spaces.
    B. She thought there would be plenty of strawberry dishes to eat, and that was her favorite fruit.
    C. She had expected Strawberry to be a bigger, more modern city.
    D. Big Ma didn't let her do anything but sit in the wagon.

10. What made Cassie yell at Mr. Barnett?
    A. She could see that a sack of flour was going to fall off the shelf onto his head, and she wanted him to get out of the way.
    B. She didn't think he should have guns on display in the front counter.
    C. He said he would only sell candy to white children.
    D. She was angry that he waited on a white child who had come in the store after them.

Roll of Thunder Multiple Choice Unit Test 2 Page 4

11. Why was Cassie mad at Big Ma?
    A. Big Ma refused to buy her candy or pretty hair ribbons.
    B. She wanted to drive the wagon home and Big Ma said no.
    C. Big Ma would not let her visit with Mr. Jamison and his family.
    D. Big Ma made her apologize to Lillian Jean.

12. Why didn't Papa want to back people's credit with his land?
    A. If the people couldn't pay their bills, he would have to sell his land for the bills he guaranteed.
    B. He didn't really like his neighbors enough to do that for them.
    C. Mama said she would not speak to him if he did it.
    D. He was afraid of what the white men might do to him.

13. What papers did Big Ma sign?
    A. An agreement to back the neighbors' credit
    B. A title transfer to give the land to Papa and Uncle Hammer
    C. A formal complaint against Mr. Simms for hurting Cassie
    D. A contract donating part of her forest to the church

14. Why did Cassie take Lillian Jean into the woods?
    A. Cassie didn't want any witnesses to see that she and Lillian Jean were fighting.
    B. Cassie planned to get Lillian Jean lost and then leave her there to scare her.
    C. There were some beautiful wildflowers that Cassie knew Lillian Jean would like to see.
    D. Cassie had built a secret tree house that she wanted to show to Lillian Jean.

15. Why did Mama lose her teaching job?
    A. There weren't enough students in the seventh grade, so the principal had to fire one teacher and put the students in another class.
    B. The school board didn't think she should be teaching in the same school that her children attended.
    C. She was not teaching what was in the history books, and she was stirring up trouble with the boycott.
    D. She was not supposed to whip the students, but she did it anyway.

16. What stopped the mob?
    A. Mr. Jamison finally convinced them he was right.
    B. The Simms boys told the truth.
    C. The sheriff and his deputies threatened to arrest them all.
    D. They all went to fight the fire in the cotton field.

Roll of Thunder Multiple Choice Unit Test 2 Page 5

III. Composition
    What things did Cassie learn in the year that passed during the events of this story? Explain your answer using examples from the story.

Roll of Thunder Multiple Choice Unit Test 2 Page 6

IV. Vocabulary   Match the words to the correct definitions.

___ 1. JOVIAL   A. hanging around with nothing particular to do

___ 2. INTERMINABLE   B. having a pleasant and friendly disposition

___ 3. OMINOUSLY   C. to caution against or warn

___ 4. CONDESCENDING   D. afflicting; troubling

___ 5. RIDICULED   E. dangerously lacking in security or stability

___ 6. EMERGED   F. descending voluntarily to the level of an inferior person

___ 7. VEX   G. something that conceals or screens like a garment

___ 8. FUMING   H. lowered in pride or dignity

___ 9. ALOOFNESS   I. unending

___ 10. CRESCENDO   J. impossible to reach or enter

___ 11. INACCESSIBLE   K. concentrating on a single purpose; engrossed

___ 12. PLAGUING   L. a gradual increase in loudness or intensity

___ 13. INTENT   M. at a distance; removed

___ 14. ADAMANTLY   N. made someone or something the object of scornful laughter

___ 15. AMIABLY   O. portentous; foreboding

___ 16. PRECARIOUSLY   P. to come forth into view

___ 17. SHROUD   Q. boiling over with anger

___ 18. LOITERING   R. boldly; not giving in; firmly

___ 19. HUMILIATED   S. to trouble or bother

___ 20. ADMONISHED   T. full of hearty, playful good humor

ANSWER SHEET - *Roll of Thunder, Hear My Cry*
Multiple Choice Unit Tests

I. Matching	II. Multiple Choice	IV. Vocabulary
1. ___	1. ___	1. ___
2. ___	2. ___	2. ___
3. ___	3. ___	3. ___
4. ___	4. ___	4. ___
5. ___	5. ___	5. ___
6. ___	6. ___	6. ___
7. ___	7. ___	7. ___
8. ___	8. ___	8. ___
9. ___	9. ___	9. ___
10. ___	10. ___	10. ___
11. ___	11. ___	11. ___
12. ___	12. ___	12. ___
13. ___	13. ___	13. ___
14. ___	14. ___	14. ___
15. ___	15. ___	15. ___
	16. ___	16. ___
		17. ___
		18. ___
		19. ___
		20. ___

ANSWER KEY MULTIPLE CHOICE UNIT TESTS
Roll of Thunder, Hear My Cry

Answers to Unit Test 1 are in the left column. Answers to Unit Test 2 are in the right column.

I. Matching	II. Multiple Choice	IV. Vocabulary
1. I M	1. A C	1. A T
2. C A	2. A B	2. O I
3. M K	3. A D	3. N O
4. G E	4. C A	4. C F
5. A C	5. B D	5. H N
6. O N	6. B C	6. E P
7. B D	7. B A	7. M S
8. E G	8. C B	8. J Q
9. K I	9. A C	9. F M
10. J L	10. B D	10. L L
11. D B	11. C D	11. T J
12. F H	12. B A	12. G D
13. N O	13. C B	13. B K
14. H F	14. C A	14. R R
15. L J	15. D C	15. D B
	16. B D	16. P E
		17. Q G
		18. S A
		19. K H
		20. I C

UNIT RESOURCE MATERIALS

BULLETIN BOARD IDEAS - *Roll of Thunder, Hear My Cry*

1. Save one corner of the board for the best of students' *Roll of Thunder, Hear My Cry* writing assignments.

2. Prepare your bulletin board with plenty of open space and some pictures of black people and white people doing various activities. have each student find a quotation relevant to race relations (as an independent assignment). have all students bring their quotations to class one day and have each student write his quotation on the bulletin board. Take time to discuss the quotations and their relevance.

3. Have each student research and write a short biography of a successful or famous black person. Post the biographies on the bulletin board for students to read. You might want to take class time to discuss the biographies. Make an effort to make sure all students do different people. I suggest posting a list where students can "sign up" their choices.

4. Take one of the word search puzzles from the extra activities section and with a marker copy it over in a large size on the bulletin board. Write the clue words to find to one side. Invite students prior to and after class to find the words and circle them on the bulletin board.

5. Do a bulletin board about careers in education, retail business, and/or farming.

6. Make a bulletin board about buying land or a home, showing the steps one must go through to make a financed purchase.

7. Make a bulletin board about the cost of living. Start with the basics of shelter and food, and include the costs of heating and electricity, clothing, insurance, gasoline, etc. Give students a good idea of what it actually costs just to live moderately well.

8. Make a bulletin board about growing up. Place pictures of people in various stages of life and write under the picture the responsibilities one has or acquires at each stage of life. For example: baby-no responsibilities, 2 year old-learns basic behavior patterns (don't throw food, don't hit other kids, etc.), 5 year old-goes to Kindergarten has to begin to conform to school rules, 10 year old-helps with chores and helps look after younger siblings, 16 year old-responsibilities of dating and being out in a car, 18 year old-political responsibilities of voting, 20 year old-semi self-sufficient at college or out in the work place, 25 year old-gets married has added responsibilities of family, etc.

9. Write several of the most significant quotations from the book onto the board on brightly colored paper.

10. Do a bulletin board about the Civil Rights movement.

EXTRA ACTIVITIES

One of the difficulties in teaching a novel is that all students don't read at the same speed. One student who likes to read may take the book home and finish it in a day or two. Sometimes a few students finish the in-class assignments early. The problem, then, is finding suitable extra activities for students.

The best thing I've found is to keep a little library in the classroom. For this unit on *Roll of Thunder, Hear My Cry*, you might check out from the school library other related books and articles about the history of race relations in Mississippi, the civil rights movement, boycotts, ways to take charge of your life, goal setting and achieving goals, peer pressure and ways to remain an individual, and being responsible. Information about careers in agriculture, education, the railroad industry, retail businesses, and the law would be helpful to some students. Other works by Mildred D. Taylor or articles of criticism about *Roll of Thunder, Hear My Cry* would also be appropriate. More information about the author would be of interest to some students.

Other things you may keep on hand are puzzles. We have made some relating directly to *Roll of Thunder, Hear My Cry* for you. Feel free to duplicate them.

Some students may like to draw. You might devise a contest or allow some extra-credit grade for students who draw characters or scenes from *Roll of Thunder, Hear My Cry*. Note, too, that if the students do not want to keep their drawings you may pick up some extra bulletin board materials this way. If you have a contest and you supply the prize (a CD or something like that perhaps), you could, possibly, make the drawing itself a non-refundable entry fee.

The pages which follow contain games, puzzles and worksheets. The keys, when appropriate, immediately follow the puzzle or worksheet. There are two main groups of activities: one group for the unit; that is, generally relating to the *Roll of Thunder, Hear My Cry* text, and another group of activities related strictly to the *Roll of Thunder, Hear My Cry* vocabulary.

Directions for these games, puzzles and worksheets are self-explanatory. The object here is to provide you with extra materials you may use in any way you choose.

MORE ACTIVITIES - *Roll of Thunder, Hear My Cry*

1. Pick a chapter or scene with a great deal of dialogue and have the students act it out on a stage. (Perhaps you could assign various scenes to different groups of students so more than one scene could be acted and more students could participate.)

2. Have students define what it means to be a "friend." Tell students to list the characteristics of a "good friend" and then give them time to think about whether or not they have those characteristics themselves.

3. Have a career counselor or social services agent come into your classroom to explain programs and avenues available to people who want to better their lives but have limited resources.

4. Have students design a book cover (front and back and inside flaps) for *Roll of Thunder, Hear My Cry.*

5. Have students design a bulletin board (ready to be put up; not just sketched) for *Roll of Thunder, Hear My Cry.*

6. Have students make a list of things that they have learned as they have grown up (so far). The list should include real facts of life that have taken away their naivete. (For example, being aware of AIDS, drugs, childnappers, etc.)

7. Take time to discuss what to do if you get stuck in a situation like T.J.'s. What other avenues of action could T.J. have taken?

8. Have a "Mississippi Day" during which you take time to do a little travelogue about the state of Mississippi, learning its location, topography, industries, interesting sights to see, historical information, etc.

9. Discuss the condition and treatment of Afro-Americans in society in the 1930's vs today.

WORD SEARCH - *Roll of Thunder, Hear My Cry*

All words in this list are associated with *Roll of Thunder, Hear My Cry*. The words are placed backwards, forward, diagonally, up and down. The included words are listed below the word searches.

```
L F H Z M D C F M G B H G W F C D N N D F N Z Q
Q F D O N I N Y F U G R C K K S O T Z I I Z N B
C F Q A L R S I Y Y T H C P E G F J H G G R Z T
S O L D I E R S G R E A T F A I T H S U B R T H
G X A U L E I A I A J C T W R P S M A X N . A M
L N K T T A N D T S Z X A E D J E S K M J D R C
D I T N D E E I S Y S N D L S L E R A . M O E N
Y I L B Y R N N J E Z I E G L T R R S C L E G R
L R L L S G O V R X C N P I R A A E E Y V U R C
Z H R F I S O O J B I R N P Y A W C A M R W A B
P J K E I A T L Q L O G E V I V N T E D Y R N P
Q N Y R B S N Y O B S Y X T N Y I G M Y E O E Y
M N R S W W J R J P N J C F S D M C E I S R X B
C O S N F L A A C V A Y M O E G N R K R S V S L
M O T W H C Q R M L C X C R T O S R E S C S Z Z
M X T P Q R L Q T I W G C Q T T M F H L B G U R
V C T T M X B V G S S H G Y M Y F K X T S U T S
F X P P O G B V S S D O A G Q E V W W N N J R M
M X L M P N F P S N J L N R J Q H W L N P K V G
Z M Z S S W G J G G C Z K N J Z K D T L R Z D D
```

APOLOGY	DIRT	LEG	SOLDIERS
BERRYS	FIRE	LILLIAN	STACEY
BOYCOTT	FIRED	LITTLE	STORE
BUS	FLUTE	MISSISSIPPI	STRAWBERRY
CAR	GRANGER	MISSUS	T.J.
CAROLINE	GREAT	FAITH	MORRISON
CASSIE	HAMMER	NIGRA	TATUM
CHEATING	HOLE	PAPERS	TAYLOR
CLAYTON	JACK	PAUL	THUNDER
COAT	JAMISON	READERS	VICKSBURG
COTTON	JEFFERSON	RIDERS	WAGON
CREDIT	JEREMY	SECRETS	WALLACE
DAISY	LAND	SMELLINGS	TAR

CROSSWORD - *Roll of Thunder, Hear My Cry*

CROSSWORD CLUES - *Roll of Thunder, Hear My Cry*

ACROSS

3. Stacey took TJ's punishment for this crime
5. Big Ma
10. It ran the children off the road
11. _____ _____ Elementary School
15. Mr. Jamison called Big Ma this
16. They were burned by a white man
17. Papa's broken limb
19. Mama was _____ for stirring up trouble
20. Lawyer friend of the Logans
23. Cassie did not want to give Lillian Jean one
24. _____ Bridge
27. The riders came to tar and feather him
29. Papa didn't want to back people's _____ with his land
33. Big Ma parked hers away from the store entrance
34. Cassie and Little man refused to take theirs; books
36. Author
37. Partner to feathers
38. What Lillian Jean told Cassie
39. _____ Jean; Cassie punched her

DOWN

1. Rich land owner
2. Jeremy gave Stacey a hand-made one
3. Stacey gave his new one to TJ
4. RW & Melvin beat him up
5. Narrator
6. In the front of the readers, black students were
7. _____ Davis; the white school
8. Little man didn't like to get it on his clothes
9. Told Mary Logan that C. & LM refused to take their books
12. This stopped the mob
13. He drove a Packard like Mr. Granger's
14. _____ Edward; Big Ma's husband
16. Mama organized one against Wallaces' store
18. The horse
21. Hammer sold his to get money for the mortgage
22. The price on this crop had dropped
25. White men who harassed black people
26. White boy friendly towards the Logans
28. Big, strong friend of the Logan Family
29. _____ Chester; Little Man
30. Logan children dug one in the road
31. Logans had 400 acres of it
32. Big Ma signed these giving title of the land to her children
35. Felt responsible for Papa's broken leg

CROSSWORD ANSWER KEY - *Roll of Thunder, Hear My Cry*

					G		F						C	H	E	A	T	I	N	G			
			C	A	R	O	L	I	N	E			O				J						
			A		A		U		I		J		A			D				D			
	B	U	S		N		T		G	R	E	A	T	F	A	I	Y	H		A		P	
			S		G		E		R		F			I		R		A		I		A	
			I		E				A		F			R		T		M	I	S	S	U	S
		B	E	R	R	Y	S			L	E	G		E				M		Y		L	
		O						J			R				F	I	R	E	D				
		Y					J	A	M	I	S	O	N					R					
C		C		C				C			O												
A	P	O	L	O	G	Y		K			N				S	O	L	D	I	E	R	S	
R		T		T						J											I		
		T	A	T	U	M		C	R	E	D	I	T						H		D		
	L			O		O		L		R							P		O		E		
W	A	G	O	N		R	E	A	D	E	R	S				T	A	Y	L	O	R		
	N					R		Y		M		T	A	R			P		E		S		
	D					I		T		Y		A					E						
						S		O				C					R						
						O		N			S	E	C	R	E	T	S						
L	I	L	L	I	A	N						Y											

MATCHING QUIZ/WORKSHEET 1 - *Roll of Thunder, Hear My Cry*

___ 1. BOYCOTT   A.   Davis; the "white" school

___ 2. GRANGER   B. _____Creek

___ 3. MISSUS   C. They were burned by a white man

___ 4. WALLACE   D. Mr. Jamison called Big Ma this

___ 5. WAGON   E. Stacey gave his new one to TJ

___ 6. GREAT FAITH   F. Wallace place forbidden to the children

___ 7. JACK   G. Logans had 400 acres of it

___ 8. LAND   H. He drove a Packard like Mr. Granger's

___ 9. BERRYS   I. Author

___ 10. STRAWBERRY   J. Rich land owner

___ 11. TAYLOR   K. Cassie did not want to give Lillian Jean one

___ 12. SECRETS   L. What Lillian Jean told Cassie

___ 13. COAT   M. Mama organized one against Wallaces' store

___ 14. JEREMY   N. Logan children dug one in the road

___ 15. JEFFERSON   O. The horse

___ 16. HOLE   P. Store Owner

___ 17. HAMMER   Q. _____ _____ Elementary School

___ 18. APOLOGY   R. White boy friendly towards the Logans

___ 19. SMELLINGS   S. Big Ma parked hers away from the store entrance

___ 20. STORE   T. Cassie was disappointed with this city

MATCHING QUIZ/WORKSHEET 2 - *Roll of Thunder, Hear My Cry*

___ 1. VICKSBURG   A. _____Creek

___ 2. LAND   B. Big Ma parked hers away from the store entrance

___ 3. NIGRA   C. _____Chester; Little Man

___ 4. FLUTE   D. The riders came to tar and feather him

___ 5. JAMISON   E. Papa's broken limb

___ 6. WAGON   F. Logan children dug one in the road

___ 7. BUS   G. It ran the children off the road

___ 8. FIRED   H. The horse

___ 9. THUNDER   I. Jeremy gave Stacey a hand-made one

___ 10. SMELLINGS   J. Cassie did not want to give Lillian Jean one

___ 11. CLAYTON   K. In the front of the readers, black students were

___ 12. STACEY   L. Logans had 400 acres of it

___ 13. CHEATING   M. Roll of _____, Hear my Cry

___ 14. DAISY   N. City where the boycotters got their food

___ 15. GRANGER   O. Lawyer friend of the Logans

___ 16. TATUM   P. Told Mary Logan that C & LM refused to take their books

___ 17. APOLOGY   Q. Felt responsible for Papa's broken leg

___ 18. HOLE   R. Rich land owner

___ 19. JACK   S. Stacey took TJ's punishment for this crime

___ 20. LEG   T. Mama was _____ for stirring up trouble

KEY: MATCHING QUIZ/WORKSHEETS - *Roll of Thunder, Hear My Cry*

Worksheet 1	Worksheet 2
1. M	1. N
2. J	2. L
3. D	3. K
4. P	4. I
5. S	5. O
6. Q	6. B
7. O	7. G
8. G	8. T
9. C	9. M
10. T	10. A
11. I	11. C
12. L	12. Q
13. E	13. S
14. R	14. P
15. A	15. R
16. N	16. D
17. H	17. J
18. K	18. F
19. B	19. H
20. F	20. E

JUGGLE LETTER REVIEW GAME CLUE SHEET - *Roll of Thunder, Hear My Cry*

SCRAMBLED	WORD	CLUE
OLOYGPA	APOLOGY	Cassie did not want to give Lillian Jean one
ACTO	COAT	Stacey gave his new one to T.J.
USB	BUS	It ran the children off the road
OOIRMNRS	MORRISON	Big, strong friend of the Logan Family
TCBTYOO	BOYCOTT	Mama organized one against Wallaces' store
KCAJ	JACK	The horse
IAH ARGTRFTE	GREAT FAITH	_____ _____ Elementary School
ELHO	HOLE	Logan children dug one in the road
ANRGI	NIGRA	In the front of the readers, black students were
RCA	CAR	Hammer sold his to get money for the mortgage
INGMSELSL	SMELLINGS	_____ Creek
NDAL	LAND	Logans had 400 acres of it
BKGSCURVI	VICKSBURG	City where the boycotters got their food
AULP	PAUL	_____Edward; Big Ma's husband
PSIPISSMIIS	MISSISSIPPI	State in which the story takes place
EOJERSFNF	JEFFERSON	_____Davis; the white school
LTEUF	FLUTE	Jeremy gave Stacey a hand-made one
YISDA	DAISY	Told Mary Logan that C. & LM refused to take their books
YACEST	STACEY	Felt responsible for Papa's broken leg
IFER	FIRE	This stopped the mob
TTUMA	TATUM	The riders came to tar and feather him
TSECRES	SECRETS	What Lillian Jean told Cassie
ART	TAR	Partner to feathers
TCTONO	COTTON	The price on this crop had dropped
OIENCRAL	CAROLINE	Big Ma
SSMUSI	MISSUS	Mr. Jamison called Big Ma this
DEIFR	FIRED	Mama was _____ for stirring up trouble
EJMRYE	JEREMY	White boy friendly towards the Logans
RICTED	CREDIT	Papa didn't want to back people's _____ with his land
IT-TLLE	LITTLE-	_____-Man; Clayton Chester
TEHCGAIN	CHEATING	Stacey took TJ's punishment for this crime
ERSYRB	BERRYS	They were burned by a white man
RSTEO	STORE	Wallace place forbidden to the children
LWAEALC	WALLACE	Store owner
EGL	LEG	Papa's broken limb
SREPPA	PAPERS	Big Ma signed these giving title of the land to her children
ESEARRD	READERS	Cassie and Little man refused to take theirs; books

VOCABULARY RESOURCE MATERIALS

VOCABULARY WORD SEARCH - *Roll of Thunder, Hear My Cry*

All words in this list are associated with *Roll of Thunder, Hear My Cry* with an emphasis on the vocabulary words chosen for study in the text. The words are placed backwards, forward, diagonally, up and down. The included words are listed below.

```
O Q V X F N T P V X W Z Z D G K G T M H R H Z D
O B V I O U S E M E R G E D I N D I G N A N T V
S Q L N N X M Z H G X N Q L I C I A S Q T Q Y P
C H S I X T N I Y Y O D A U B C R R M E X J F D
F O R C V B E L N D J A G P D A R E E I I T E L
T E N O O I T N N G M A D Y P Y N D S T A Z G N
D F I T U N O O T O L U L M L R E I E C I B E Q
I I Q G A D C U P P I S T S O T E J M N E O L Y
S N C M N G D E S H U T U E A N D H O R N N L Y
R Z A A E E I Q S O E O A I L E I R E V E U D W
P D M C L N D O N S I N L R G Y T S D N I T H O
A J E B C P A I U R I I O N E A R E H D S A N S
Z Y M T H E M C A S M O U M P P T W E E G I L I
B A V R N O S C I U B L N N E A S L G N D R V D
S C S J W U E S H N V V G H I N U A I C V L L E
T Z F D D R A G I R G J V L W C A L X L C H H J
T R F W P N Y D T B C L A Q I F G L J E H B M G
T Y G C P K H M N B L T Y D Q N P T X Q V Z W N
T F N F F N G G C U E E I N I A L O O F N E S S
X N Q P V V S M V R P R R M J K Y P X G T P L P
```

ADAMANTLY	EMERGED	LOITERING	PLACID
ADMONISHED	EXASPERATION	LUNGED	PLAGUING
ALOOFNESS	FEIGNED	MENACINGLY	PRECARIOUSLY
AMBLED	FUMING	MINGLING	RETALIATED
AMIABLY	HUMILIATED	MUTELY	RIDICULED
APPREHENSIVE	INACCESSIBLE	OBLIVIOUS	SEIZE
CONCESSION	INDIGNANT	OBVIOUS	SHROUD
CONDONED	INTENT	OMINOUSLY	SHUNNED
CONTAGIOUS	INTERMINABLE	PATRONIZE	UNDAUNTED
CRESCENDO	JOVIAL	PHENOMENAL	VEX

VOCABULARY CROSSWORD - *Roll of Thunder, Hear My Cry*

VOCABULARY CROSSWORD CLUES - *Roll of Thunder, Hear My Cry*

ACROSS
1. _____ Man; Clayton Chester
3. having a pleasant and friendly disposition
6. full of hearty, playful good humor
8. boldly; not giving in; firmly
11. Logans had 400 acres of it
12. to trouble or bother
13. cow sound
14. crooked; not straight
16. partner to feathers
17. endorsed; gave approval for
19. _____ Edward; Big Ma's husband
20. pretended
21. a compromise
24. to grasp; arrest
26. threateningly
27. white men who harassed black people
28. distress signal
30. contraction for cannot
31. Papa's broken limb
32. this stopped the mob
34. ignored; kept out of association with
36. the riders came to tar and feather him
38. slang for father
39. opposite of tight
41. hanging around with nothing particular to do
42. opposite of yes
43. Little Man didn't like to get it on his clothes
46. suddenly thrust
47. told Mary Logan that C. & LM refused to take their books
48. Logan children dug one in the road

DOWN
1. _____ Jean; Cassie punched her
2. RW & Melvin beat him up
4. concentrating on a single purpose; engrossed
5. Hammer sold his to get money for the mortgage
7. easy to see or understand
8. to caution against or warn
9. at a distance; removed
10. moved at a smooth, easy gait
15. unending
17. descending voluntarily to the level of an inferior person
18. lowered in pride or dignity
20. boiling over with anger
21. a gradual increase in loudness or intensity
22. impossible to reach or enter
23. not faltering or hesitating
25. feeling anger at something unjust
29. Jeremy gave Stacey a hand-made one
33. to come forth into view
35. him
37. without speaking
40. Wallace place forbidden to the children
44. unusual; peculiar
45. It ran the children off the road

VOCABULARY CROSSWORD ANSWER KEY - *Roll of Thunder, Hear My Cry*

	L	I	T	T	L	E		A	M	I	A	B	L	Y				C		
	I		J						N				J	O	V	I	A	L		
	L		A	D	A	M	A	N	T	L	Y			B				R		
	L	A	N	D		L			M	E				V	E	X				
	I		M	O	O		B	E	N	T			I		I					
T	A	R		O		O	L	T		C	O	N	D	O	N	E	D		H	
	N		N		F		E			O		T		U				P	A	U	L
		F	E	I	G	N	E	D		C	O	N	C	E	S	S	I	O	N		M
		U		S		E		R		D		R		N		O		U		I
		M		H		S	E	I	Z	E		E	M	E	N	A	C	I	N	G	L	Y
	R	I	D	E	R	S		N		S	O	S		I			C		D		I
F		N		D			D		C	A	N	T		C			A		A	
L	E	G				F	I	R	E		E		A			E		U		T
U					E		G		N		N		B			S	H	U	N	N	E	D
T	A	T	U	M		M		N		D	A	D		L	O	O	S	E		T		D
E				U		E		A		O		I		E			I			E		S
	L	O	I	T	E	R	I	N	G		N	O			B			D	I	R	T
O				E		G		T			G		B		L						O
D				L		E					L	U	N	G	E	D					R
D	A	I	S	Y		D							S					H	O	L	E

VOCABULARY WORKSHEET 1 - *Roll of Thunder, Hear My Cry*

___ 1. Impossible to reach or enter
    A. inaccessible   B. precariously   C. obvious   D. apprehensive

___ 2. Suddenly thrust
    A. plaguing   B. vulnerability   C. condescending   D. lunged

___ 3. Lowered in pride or dignity
    A. contagious   B. interminable   C. phenomenal   D. humiliated

___ 4. Unaware of; not mindful of
    A. exasperation   B. loitering   C. intent   D. oblivious

___ 5. Descending voluntarily to the level of an inferior person
    A. condescending   B. feigned   C. emerged   D. shunned

___ 6. Full of hearty, playful good humor
    A. inaccessible   B. jovial   C. indignant   D. contagious

___ 7. To grasp; arrest
    A. seize   B. jovial   C. crescendo   D. retaliated

___ 8. A compromise
    A. condoned   B. concession   C. feigned   D. intent

___ 9. Afflicting; troubling
    A. plaguing   B. obvious   C. interminable   D. precariously

___ 10. Irritation or annoyance
    A. indignant   B. exasperation   C. aloofness   D. emerged

___ 11. Ignored; kept out of association with
    A. shroud   B. placid   C. shunned   D. menacingly

___ 12. Concentrating on a single purpose; engrossed
    A. phenomenal   B. intent   C. contagious   D. placid

___ 13. At a distance; removed
    A. indignant   B. inaccessible   C. undaunted   D. aloofness

___ 14. A gradual increase in loudness or intensity
    A. vex   B. contagious   C. crescendo   D. precariously

___ 15. To trouble or bother
    A. admonished   B. vex   C. inaccessible   D. indignant

___ 16. Tranquil; calm
    A. crescendo   B. undaunted   C. placid   D. concession

___ 17. Able or quick to understand
    A. inaccessible   B. emerged   C. menacingly   D. apprehensive

___ 18. Boiling over with anger
    A. fuming   B. retaliated   C. placid   D. lunged

___ 19. To caution against or warn
    A. indignant   B. emerged   C. admonished   D. shunned

___ 20. Without speaking
    A. mingling   B. placid   C. seize   D. mutely

VOCABULARY WORKSHEET 2 - *Roll of Thunder, Hear My Cry*

___ 1. MUTELY

___ 2. ADMONISHED

___ 3. JOVIAL

___ 4. INACCESSIBLE

___ 5. INTERMINABLE

___ 6. RIDICULED

___ 7. CONTAGIOUS

___ 8. SHUNNED

___ 9. UNDAUNTED

___ 10. INDIGNANT

___ 11. MINGLING

___ 12. RETALIATED

___ 13. OMINOUSLY

___ 14. CRESCENDO

___ 15. CONCESSION

___ 16. AMBLED

___ 17. FUMING

___ 18. APPREHENSIVE

___ 19. EXASPERATION

___ 20. ADAMANTLY

A. portentous; foreboding

B. mixing together

C. boldly; not giving in; firmly

D. without speaking

E. made someone or something the object of scornful laughter

F. a compromise

G. full of hearty, playful good humor

H. not faltering or hesitating

I. easily transmitted; catching

J. irritation or annoyance

K. moved at a smooth, easy gait

L. able or quick to understand

M. a gradual increase in loudness or intensity

N. ignored; kept out of association with

O. impossible to reach or enter

P. unending

Q. boiling over with anger

R. to caution against or warn

S. returned like for like

T. feeling anger at something unjust

KEY: VOCABULARY WORKSHEETS - *Roll of Thunder, Hear My Cry*

Worksheet 1	Worksheet 2
1. A	1. D
2. D	2. R
3. D	3. G
4. D	4. O
5. A	5. P
6. B	6. E
7. A	7. I
8. B	8. N
9. A	9. H
10. B	10. T
11. C	11. B
12. B	12. S
13. B	13. A
14. C	14. M
15. B	15. F
16. C	16. K
17. D	17. Q
18. A	18. L
19. C	19. J
20. D	20. C

VOCABULARY JUGGLE LETTER REVIEW GAME CLUES
Roll of Thunder, Hear My Cry

SCRAMBLED	WORD	CLUE
NPLUGGIA	PLAGUING	anything that afflicts or troubles
OOSESALNF	ALOOFNESS	at a distance; removed
NDNESDGCICNOE	CONDESCENDING	to descend voluntarily to the level of someone or something inferior
DNGLUE	LUNGED	a sudden thrust
LAEOPNEMNH	PHENOMENAL	extremely unusual
EDEGRME	EMERGED	to come forth into view
OCDEDONN	CONDONED	forgiven
TNUUEDDNA	UNDAUNTED	not faltering or hesitating
NGRETOLII	LOITERING	hanging loosely
HNSEDNU	SHUNNED	kept away from
ATITAELEDR	RETALIATED	to return like for like
NOYUMILOS	OMINOUSLY	threateningly
IGINGNML	MINGLING	to bring or mix together
AYVRLLITUNBIE	VULNERABILITY	that can be injured or wounded
DOHRSU	SHROUD	a cloth sometimes used to wrap a corpse for burial
EZSIE	SEIZE	to grasp; or arrest
LTUYME	MUTELY	not speaking
CIPDAL	PLACID	undisturbed; tranquil
TINNAGDNI	INDIGNANT	to be displeased at; feeling anger or scorn
EZIPTOANR	PATRONIZE	to go to regularly as a customer
XVE	VEX	to trouble or bother
OAIVLJ	JOVIAL	full of hearty, playful good humor
EITDUHLAMI	HUMILIATED	lowered in pride or dignity
NLMIACGNYE	MENACINGLY	threateningly
EUPLRSACYROI	PRECARIOUSLY	dangerously lacking in security or stability
OSREXPNTAAEI	EXASPERATION	irritation or annoyance
VEEASNRPIPEH	APPREHENSIVE	able or quick to understand
IIVULOSBO	OBLIVIOUS	unaware of; not mindful of
NAISTOUGCO	CONTAGIOUS	easily transmitted; catching
AANYDMLTA	ADAMANTLY	boldly; not giving in; firmly
IAAMLYB	AMIABLY	having a pleasant and friendly disposition
ENSOECRCD	CRESCENDO	a gradual increase in loudness or intensity
IVOOSBU	OBVIOUS	easy to see or understand
MBNLARTINEIE	INTERMINABLE	unending
SEOADMINDH	ADMONISHED	cautioned against or warned
DURELIIDC	RIDICULED	made someone the object of scornful laughter

www.ingramcontent.com/pod-product-compliance
Lightning Source LLC
Chambersburg PA
CBHW051416070526
44584CB00023B/3455